Communism 2.0
25 Years Later

Dr. Ileana Johnson Paugh

ISBN-10:0692386203
ISBN-13:9780692386200

DEDICATION

I dedicate this book to my Mom, Niculina Apostolescu, who helped me complete my education by caring for my family in America when I was preoccupied with college, classes, and exams. As an excellent homemaker, she dedicated her life to caring for younger siblings, my Dad, me, her granddaughters, and my husband.

CONTENTS

ACKNOWLEDGMENTS

This book could not exist without the love and patience of my husband who provided his computer expertise, time, and broad knowledge. His love of books is always an inspiration. He is my enabler and hero who brings interesting topics to my attention.

Preface

Where do I start my journey back? It has been 25 years since communism went underground in 1989 to re-group, re-emerging around the world as a global force under the guise of progressivism and environmentalism, championed by American academics and the much disliked United Nations. The Soviet Union has been dismantled and rebuilt into one large Mother Russia and many smaller countries formerly under the umbrella of the mighty Soviet Empire.

I escaped communism in 1978 and built a life in the most exceptional nation on earth where freedom and opportunity were not just empty promises. I am watching perplexed every day how the free America I so loved is now turning into a communist country willingly from within.

The population seems mesmerized by the empty communist promise of equality and social justice and Americans are eager to destroy the best medical care in the world for a very expensive and unaffordable nationalized socialist health system where rationing and often substandard care are the norm.

School and college professors have convinced generations of young people that the only perfect society is communism and the faster we get there, the more prosperous America will be. Apparently we have been quite evil and shameful so far in our capitalist greed while we freed and improved the lot of so many nations around the world with our free market. The lessons of history are already forgotten.

We are changing rapidly into a crony capitalist state led by a political and economic oligarchy that is stealing our wealth and hard work and redistributing it with impunity to the undeserving and to illegal aliens while the elites in power keep their billions intact and hidden from confiscatory taxation.

We are at a cross roads where we have less liberty in America than the freedom I found in the former Iron Curtain countries. Twenty-five years after the Berlin wall was dismantled and communism was declared dead, it is re-emerging with a vengeance in an altered state, a Communism 2.0, a version with elements of crony capitalism, a nouveau society ruled by the former communist party oligarchy, much more powerful and wealthier than before, having sold the unprofitable former enterprises and factories that belonged to the people under the Soviet regime. In the absence of law and order and in the presence of mass confusion, nobody was held accountable for the huge theft on a national scale, and a few oligarchs amassed huge fortunes from selling state property and re-investing it in enterprises with western partners or banking the cash. People's lives improved for a while until the 2008 mortgage crisis in the west which sent shock waves around the world and around the entire European Union membership, reeling from the economic collapse. The elderly, who became the most neglected segment of the population, began to feel nostalgia for the old days of communism when the meager existence of a controlled slave was more desirable than the uncertainty of a free market where humans were required to actually be responsible for their own survival instead of depending on the mighty government largesse.

"We've Proven that Communism Works"

I am not really that surprised that young people are enamored of communism. Their teachers have been indoctrinating them for years into the utopia of "social justice," "environmental justice," the "evil" middle class, and the spectacular equality for all as envisioned by Marx, Engels, and Lenin.

Communism is "cool" in the land where wearing a Che Guevara t-shirt is a hypocritical political statement made while enjoying capitalist amenities. But we expect them to mature eventually and give up the absurdity that communism has not succeeded because the wrong people were in charge.

Furthermore, we don't expect them to elect representatives that mirror their youthful ignorance. Rep. Joe Garcia, a Democrat from Florida, said, trying to explain our "broken immigration system" that needs to be fixed by enacting comprehensive immigration reform, "Two of the safest cities in America, two of them are on the border with Mexico. And of course, the reason is we've proved that communism works. If you give everybody a good, government job, there's no crime. But that isn't what we should be doing on the border."

He tried to walk back the outrageous statement by saying, "My grandfather died under house arrest in Cuba. I'm under no illusions of what evil is." Apparently he does have some explaining to do how 100 million innocents died through mass starvation, executions, imprisonment in gulags (re-education and forced labor camps), beatings, and torture at the hands of communist rulers during the 20th century, and how Cubans and North Koreans still suffer today under totalitarian communist regimes.

Communism promoters may want to explain what is happening now in South Africa under a Marxist-Leninist regime where the South African Communist Party (SAPC) plans to pursue the "radical second phase" of the ongoing communist revolution, confiscation of private property and businesses.[1]

Perhaps Hollywood, the main stream media, and academic progressives in this country who worship at the altar of communism and wish to transform our country into a communist "paradise" should explain how the dear leaders elevate themselves to god-like status and expect total worship from their subjects, even in their homes, the huge self-portraits and statues erected everywhere, a dangerous cult of personality, the glorification and celebration of the dear leader who replaces the parents of every child in the country, and how communists destroyed the middle class and killed intellectuals.

Can the influential elite explain to us Lenin's secret police force, Cheka, established to eliminate dissent through execution and forced relocation to hard labor camps? It served as a model for other police force bodies in Soviet satellite countries. How about the executive orders Lenin wrote to shoot or hang kulaks (wealthy peasants), priests, and other "harmful insects?" How can anyone say that communism was or is good? Gone were religion, freedom of speech, private gun ownership, land ownership, food, medicine, decent housing, shelter, and clothes.

Viewed from space at night, North Korea looks pitch-black, but the rest of the world is illuminated. Billions are spent to support the dear leader's cult of personality while the population suffers and exists in a suspended state of malnutrition. If anybody protests, North Korea has "Camp 22" forced labor encampment which holds in excess of 50,000 people.

Fidel Castro and Che Guevara brought communism to Latin America. Over 100,000 Cubans have fled Castro's regime and an estimated 15,000-18,000 had been killed by the Castro government. During fifty years of repressive rule, Castro destroyed property rights, freedom of speech, press, assembly, put on show trials to dispose of enemies, banned Christmas, and built a prison camp to lock away those labeled "enemies of the state" who disagreed with him - poets, priests, journalists, nuns, dissenters/activists, and homosexuals.

Che Guevara, Castro's chief advisor, left in 1965 to train communists in Africa and Bolivia. Che was not successful in Africa and was executed in 1967 by government forces in Bolivia. However, the current Bolivian president, Evo Morales, "redistributed land and nationalized key industries, expressing his belief that 'he [Che] inspires us to continue fighting, changing not only Bolivia, but all of Latin America and the world.'"[2]

Paul Kengor described how Venezuela was radically transformed by Hugo Chavez, a Castro ally. He nationalized industries, redistributed land, and censored the main stream media. Medical care was nationalized, and people suffered under his rule. The communist Shining Path guerrillas killed close to 35,000 Peruvians. Daniel Ortega, President of Nicaragua, trained in Cuba to become the leader of the Sandinistas, the communists who overthrew the government in 1979, and who nationalized industries and redistributed the land. "Since 2007 Ortega adopted a policy of democratic socialism."

Perhaps progressives can explain to the rest of the American voters who are lulled into a false sense of security by clever rhetoric and euphemisms, the construction of the Berlin Wall in 1961 and its existence until November 9, 1989.

Nikita Khrushchev and Walter Ulbricht gave orders and, on August 13, 1961, the construction of the infamous wall of shame made of concrete and barbed wire began. The Berlin Wall was a glaring expression for 28 years of communist repression which restricted the freedom of movement of its citizens. Those living under communism became "captives" overnight, cut off from the rest of the world while some family members lived free on the opposite side of the street and of the wall.

"For half a century, nearly all of Eastern and Central Europe suffered under communist rule." Poland, Czechoslovakia, Hungary, Estonia, Latvia, Lithuania, Romania, Bulgaria, and Yugoslavia fell one by one under the rule and influence of the Soviet regime.

After 1989, a host of changes took place, the European Union was formed, 27 countries gave up their monetary policy power to bureaucrats in Brussels, the environmental lobby became very powerful in their quest to protect earth from a manufactured global warming crisis, the communists went underground to regroup and emerged more powerful and stealthy around the world, taking over slowly through academic indoctrination, with the help of crony capitalist millionaires and billionaires.

The illegal immigrants who are currently in our country and who are sending their young through coyotes via Mexico come from Latin and Central American countries where dictatorship, repression, and corruption are the norm. They do not understand any other form of rule and therefore vote, legally or illegally, for the same type of failed society which they've escaped from, either socialist or communist. Lenin's Bolsheviks would be proud – his dream of a world-wide workers' paradise may commence under the leadership of a one world elite government guided by the borderless United Nations.

Communism Then and Now

"We now live in a nation where doctors destroy health, lawyers destroy justice, universities destroy knowledge, governments destroy freedom, the press destroys information, religion destroys morals, and our banks destroy the economy." – Chris Hedges

"There is no difference between communism and socialism, except in the way of achieving the same ultimate goal: communism proposes to enslave men by force, socialism by voting. It's the same difference between murder and suicide." - Ayn Rand

A pamphlet published by Alfred G. Meyer at Harvard in 1953, and designed to teach young people about the subversion and evils of communism, revealed that "communists in disguise have slipped into influential places in our country." At that time, the movement was modest, with little influence, and a membership of 35,000 people, about 1/50 of one percent of the population. At its membership height, there were around 200,000 communists in the U.S. It is hard to estimate a number today, however, judging by those who are constantly in the limelight and voting for communist policies, the numbers are growing.

Membership and influence is growing because the New York based Communist Party USA's rhetoric appeals to the lowest common denominator, to those who are already on welfare, illegal aliens, and permanent residents coming from third world dictatorships, and union members who are controlled by communist leaders. A constant and highly successful propaganda is waged by the Democrat Party and progressive elites, using the communist slogans of "hope and change," "forward," "social justice," "environmental justice," "white-privilege," and "income inequality."

Communists appear so successful because Americans have a short collective memory, short attention span, and know, thanks to a socialist academia, very little of their own non-revisionist history, and even less world history. College graduates are hard-pressed to answer correctly basic questions about history, geography, and government. Yet they know what the latest Hollywood celebrity ate for supper yesterday. The main stream media, academia, and Hollywood are the main propaganda arm of mass indoctrination, comprised of "useful idiots," a term coined and used by Stalin.

Saul Alinsky described in his book, *Rules for Radicals*, the eight levels of control necessary to create a socialist regime. **Healthcare, welfare** (food, housing, income), and **education** must be controlled by the state. **Religion** must be made irrelevant by removing it from government and schools. **Guns** must be confiscated in order to create a police state. Create as much **poverty** as possible. Poor people are easier to control. Explode **national debt** to unsustainable levels by out of control spending fueled by new and suffocating taxes that create more poverty. Use escalating **class warfare** rhetoric to fuel the division between "rich" and "poor," causing discontent. Malcontent would then drive the welfare poor to rebel against the "greedy rich" who "do not pay their fair share," and to demand that they be taxed more.

How did people get ahead under the former communist Soviet-ruled Iron Curtain?

They became members of the communist party and their sympathizers, and displayed their loyalty by copying and emulating everything Marxists did. They made themselves useful by spying on other people, on their own relatives, on their own immediate families, reporting to the thought and economic police on their activities, and through loyal nepotism.

How did people get ahead in our former Constitutional Republic? Americans excelled through hard work, long hours, study, sacrifices, risk-taking through entrepreneurship, and education. Now they get ahead through crony capitalism, nepotism, corruption, strict adherence to the Democrat Party platform, race baiting, claiming faux discrimination, invoking the manufactured and non-existent "white privilege," using oppressed minority claims, lawsuits, socialist and environmentalist brainwashing in public schools, and radicalism wrapped in extreme feminism and homosexual rights.

Karl Marx wrote about capitalism as a conflict between the wealthy factory owners (the capitalists) and the proletariat (workers who had to toil for the capitalist in order to survive). Marx, a leech himself, wrote that capitalists took advantage of the proletariat. He attempted to explain that "as long as capitalism existed, the misery of mankind would grow greater." To solve this problem, "workers would rise and start a revolution that would bring comfort and control over their lives and jobs." We know this took place across the former Soviet-led communist countries with disastrous results – the workers became much poorer, more miserable, more oppressed, living in a totalitarian regime, while their communist handlers became richer by stealing "communal property."

The followers of Marx (a bum supported financially by rich friends) split into two camps: the socialists (those willing to reform capitalism) and the communists (those willing to destroy capitalism). The "soft Marxists," called in Russia "Mensheviks," preached for a slow pace to learning self-governing. The "hard Marxists," Bolsheviks/communists led by Vladimir Ilich Lenin, believed men were not disciplined enough to grow, they had to be forced into revolution. Lenin is considered the first Soviet dictator, and Joseph Stalin, who came to power after Lenin died, the second dictator.

After bloody struggles such as the Civil War in Russia, 1918-1921, the rebuilding and arguing period, 1921-1928, the first five-year plan, 1928-1932, and unprecedented progress in building a modern industrial empire between 1932-1953, Russia became a country admired by "people in India, Africa, and China."[3]

Having lived under socialism/communism, I know from first-hand experience that five-year plans were a joke. We constantly struggled to find basics because not enough finished goods and food were produced to satisfy demand. For example, a Soviet factory that was scheduled to produce 50,000 tractors in 1930, managed to build only 3,000. The factory received the "Order of the Camel" for "breaks in the plan and wastage."

The important questions about communism are:

1. Was there equality and democracy under communism?
2. Did everyone experience the same and equal quality of life and "the good things of life?"
3. Was the struggle between classes non-existent?
4. Were classes really abolished forever?

The short answer to all of the above questions is no. The complex answer is that communist countries were ruled by the Communist Party Presidium. There was no middle class, only the proletariat and the ruling communist elite. Everyone worked for equally meager pay, regardless of skill, training, or education, and for the government, which was staffed only with communist party leaders.

The Five-Year Plan was draconian, covered the entire communist nation, and the workers were either not equipped, did not have enough resources, skill, machinery, were wasteful, or not sufficiently trained or paid to meet the outlandish demands. If the plan was not met, the worker's pay was cut drastically. If waste and fraud were found, the person in charge who did not necessarily commit the crime, went to jail for economic failures of duty. If the worker exceeded the Five-Year Plan requirements, large bonuses were given, but the standards were also raised, making it impossible to meet them again. To get materials in the attempt to fulfill the plan, people resorted to theft, black market deals, swindles, and bribery, making the Five-Year Plan rather "disorderly" and mismanaged.

As a police state, there were three organizations that ruled any communist country--administrators who ran the affairs of the country, the Communist Party who gave directives for national policy and publicity from its centralized position, and the political police that watched over the communist loyalty and compliance of the citizenry.

If you think such a practice of loyalty watch and speech compliance is dead, consider the city of Barcelona, from the state of Catalonia, Spain, who created the "Anti-rumor Agency" and certified 436 "anti-rumor" volunteer agents to catch and punish those whose beliefs are not in line with the "consensus," with "groupthink." "The agents will patrol the streets, butt into certain conversations, and spread politically correct information."[4]

"Groupthink" is the "consensus" established and highly publicized through the main stream media by self-appointed moral know-it-alls, suppressing any evidence that might question the "consensus," stereotyping, demonizing, and denigrating anyone with a divergent opinion or view.

Anyone who questions and disagrees with the global warming/climate change or any other "consensus" is a "denier," "flat-Earther," "creationist," "xenophobe," "homophobe," "bigot," "racist," or "fascist." Charles Krauthammer reported in his "Thought Police on Patrol" how 110,000 individuals signed a petition to "his newspaper not to carry any more articles questioning the fact of man-made global warming."[5]

Professors who dared buck the system were fired from left-leaning academia after decades of scientific work.

In 1953, the Assistant Director of the Russian Research Center at Harvard University, Alfred G. Meyer, advised Americans how to fight world communism as an existential threat. The first threat was the "powerful war machine." The second threat was "the possibility that communist propaganda will convert people of the free nations to the Marxist cause."[6]

Sixty years later it appears that the world communist movement is taking roots in the U.S. quite nicely from within, lured and supported by the constant main stream media propaganda machine.

Alfred Meyer posed an interesting question in 1953 which rings true today in light of developing "thought police" around the world. "How does the attempt to silence ideas by punishing people who hold them square with the American traditions of civil liberties? How can we remain democratic if any set of ideas is declared illegal?" In the latest developments, patriotic, Christian, pro-American, pro-Constitution ideals, ideas, and our freedom of speech have been attacked under the rubric of "hate speech." Is it really effective to punish and destroy people who hold ideas and ideals different from yours?

Is it not despicable to prey on people's "feelings" of poverty, economic inequality and insecurity (caused by the administrations' economic policies) by promoting the utopia of communism as a desirable alternative to the "failed and unjust" capitalism?

People, who are ignorant and frightened every day by the main stream media, buy into communist dogma, slogans, and rhetoric. Illegals are an easy sell because they don't know anything else but tyranny and are enchanted by the generous welfare that, they think, comes from the ever full government coffers. Minorities who are told every day they have been slighted by prejudice and injustice buy into the deliberately deceptive communist rhetoric as well.

Inequality and injustice cannot be wiped out by destroying one successful economic model and replacing it with a failed economic model just because some charismatic promoter says it will succeed this time because the right people are in charge. At the end of the day, communism is still a form of totalitarianism no matter how you slice it.

Communism Revisited - Program of the Communist Party of the Soviet Union

"Communism is Soviet power plus the electrification of the whole country." This is Lenin's formula as quoted by the Communist Party Program of the Soviet Union on page 62.

The draft of the Program of the Communist Party of the Soviet Union was presented to the Communist Party's Twenty-Second Congress in October 1961. Crosscurrents Press in New York published it in English "as an aid to everyone wanting to understand the plans and intentions of those who lead and govern the Soviet Union." It was a time when the Cold War highlighted the existential fight between communism and capitalism, separated by an invisible red line in the sand.[7]

The communist platform emphasized the phrase "scientific communism," with contrived stages of development in an attempt to give it a scientific facade. Communism, as a concept and linguistically derived from the Latin word "communis" (shared) is neither scientific nor "shared."

The theory of scientific communism had to be developed and propagandized and the Communist education had to be improved.[8]

Public education was required to prepare citizens for vocations needed by the communist society. Children were to be molded into "harmoniously developed members of Communist society" and the "elimination of substantial distinctions between mental and physical labor." The principles of the "Communist outlook" were to be taught and school children were to be engaged in "socially useful labor to the extent of their physical capacity."[9]

The parental influence of their children's education had to be **harmonized** with "their public upbringing." Schools were meant to inculcate not just "love of labor and of knowledge in children" but also "to raise the younger generation into the spirit of Communist consciousness and morality."[10]

Literature and art had to be "imbued with optimism and dynamic Communist ideas." [11]

Collectivism was highly encouraged and **the cult of the individual** was discouraged.[12]

The Party's banner was inscribed, "From each according to his ability, to each according to his needs." The Party's motto was "Everything in the name of man, for the benefit of man" and the militant slogan proclaimed, "Workers of all countries, unite!"[13]

In case there was any doubt that the socialist world was expanding and the capitalist world was cut down to size, the program proclaimed that "Socialism will inevitably succeed capitalism everywhere" because it is the "objective law of social development."

When communism eventually accomplished its mission, the Soviets said, there will be no social inequality, no oppression, no exploitation, no war, just "peace, labor, freedom, equality, and happiness on earth." I wondered how the 100 million innocents worldwide, who were killed by communists, would have responded to such empty and meaningless rhetoric.

"Capitalism extensively exploits female and child labor."[14]

Before this document was published, child labor was a thing of the past in the United States, and women comprised 29.6 percent of the labor force in 1950. Many women stayed home to raise their children and care for their families.[15]

Communists, under the leadership of Lenin, "worked out a plan for the **radical transformation** of the country, for the construction of socialism." The plan had three prongs: the industrialization of the country, agricultural cooperation, and the Cultural Revolution.

Industrialization

As those who lived through socialism can attest, forced industrialization into a large scale modern industry resulted in an impoverished populace who survived on the crumbs left after a lot of funds and natural resources, that should have been earmarked for improving the population's standard of living, were used to industrialize a poorly run centralized economy that wasted a lot of resources.

The program of the Communist Party proposed the development of a first-class heavy industry, defense, and services for the population in the areas of "trade, public catering, health, housing, and communal services." As we well know, life under communism was very brutal in every aspect.

Total industrial output proposed was to exceed in 10 years 150 percent of the 1961 level of the U.S. industrial output and in 20 years by 500 percent, leaving the U.S. far behind. This was to be accomplished by raising productivity in ten years by 100 percent and by 300-350 percent within 20 years. The goals are laughable today just as they were in 1961.[16]

Major economic areas were set up in the Urals, the Volga, Siberia, Transcaucasia, the Baltic area, and Central Asia and production planning was centrally done.[17]

Labor productivity was supposed to increase in agriculture through the kolkhoz (collectives) system as charted by Vladimir I. Lenin by merging kolkhoz property and individual property into one Communist property. Productivity was to increase 150 percent in ten years and then 5-6 times more in the following ten years. That certainly never happened. Machinery, spare parts, and repair know-how were lacking and the young agricultural labor force tended to seek employment in cities for better opportunities.[18]

Agricultural Cooperation

Agricultural cooperation meant that everyone had to give up their land for the **common good**, willingly or by force, with no compensation whatsoever, and form cooperative farms from which the communists derived the lion's share of income from crops, cattle, pigs, horses, and chicken. Peasants were lucky to escape with their lives and the clothes on their backs, and very fortunate to survive the forced move into high-rise concrete block apartments located in very crowded cities.

"Millions of small individual farms went into **voluntary** associations to form collective farms." Large-scale "socialist farming" predicated on confiscated land destroyed the formerly plentiful crops of each individual family who brought home the fruits of their labor. Now each family had to be content with the leftovers after the Party claimed their planned lion's share.

Cultural Revolution

The Cultural Revolution included the forced indoctrination and re-education in labor camps of those who resisted communism: "skeptics, capitulators, Trotskyists, Right opportunists, nationalist-deviators, and other hostile groups." [19]

To achieve this Cultural Revolution, illiteracy had to be wiped out. The socialist intelligentsia was created through indoctrination and the so-called classless society was now comprised of workers, peasants, and intellectuals, all ruled from the top by the communist party elites.

The ridiculous idea that now citizens have a material interest in the fruits of their labor was expressed in the motto, "we pretend to work and they pretend to pay us." They never raised the people's standard of living as they claimed, on the contrary, they impoverished the former well-off farmers whose land they confiscated.

There was never an awareness that workers labored for themselves and society. The awareness was that everyone worked for the government bureaucrats who were beholden and answered to the communist party elites.

Although freedom of speech, press, and assembly were written in the Constitution which was often revised, nobody lived under the false sense of being able to speak their minds without disappearing the very next day and never to be seen again.

Because the Socialist revolution "established the dictatorship of the proletariat," 100 nations and nationalities lived **harmoniously** within the USSR. At least that is what the propaganda led you to believe. The only dictatorship the Eastern European block has experienced has been the dictatorship of the Communist Party elite and its chosen dear leader.

"The Socialist reorganization of society" has been so successful, claimed the Communist Party's program, that "The highroad to Socialism has been paved. Many peoples are already marching along it, and it will be taken sooner or later by all peoples."[20]

"The countries of the Socialist system have accumulated considerable collective experience in the remolding of the lives of hundreds of millions of people." [21]

I can personally attest to this **remolding** of our lives. We were comfortable and had a home one day and the next day we lost everything to the new communist regime. Several family members went into gulags for being "bourgeois," some survived, some did not, property was confiscated, everyone was impoverished overnight, savings and personal belongings were taken, and everyone was forcefully re-educated into the **cult of personality** and adulation of the president and his wife Elena.

According to the Program of the Communist Party of the Soviet Union, the Socialists had in common:

- Same type of economy based on the social ownership of the means of production
- Same type of political system based on the rule of the people led by the working class
- Same Marxist-Leninist ideology

- Same defense against the "imperialist camp"
- Same common goal of communism. [22]

Communists believed that their number one responsibility was to educate the "working people" in the vein of "internationalism, Socialist patriotism, and **intolerance** of all possible manifestations of nationalism and chauvinism. Nationalism is harmful to the common interests of the Socialist community."[23]

It is now easy to understand the planned drive to erase national borders and sovereignty that have previously defined successful western nations with free market capitalist economies. "Bourgeois nationalism" and "national egoism" are vehemently opposed, however, "Communists always show utmost consideration for the national feelings of the masses."[24]

It is interesting to note how much money, force, police, and military might the Communist Party employed to keep the masses from escaping the borders of the impoverished, poorly-run and spirit-suffocating socialist states, heavily guarded by devoted and brain-washed apparatchiks and well-paid informants. The East Germans even built the Berlin Wall between them and their West German brothers and sisters who believed in freedom. The wall was built not to keep people from coming in but to keep people from escaping communism.

The Soviets stated that World War I and the October Revolution caused a general crisis of capitalism. Part two of its crisis began with World War II and the Socialist revolution. "World capitalism has now entered a new, third stage of that crisis, the principal feature of which is that its development is not tied to a world war."[25]

In their 1961 opinion, world wars, economic crises, the military industrial complex, and political unrest accelerated the transformation of "monopoly capitalism into state-monopoly capitalism."

"The oppression of finance capital keeps growing. Giant monopolies controlling the bulk of social production dominate the life of the nation. A handful of millionaires and multi-millionaires (make that billionaires today) wield arbitrary power over the entire wealth of the capitalist world and make the life of entire nations mere small change in their selfish deals. The financial oligarchy is getting fabulously rich."[26] Of course they left out the Communist Party elites who were also getting offensively rich at the expense of the proletariat. The paragraph contains eerily similar developments today.

"The state is becoming a committee for the management of the affairs of the monopoly bourgeoisie. The bureaucratization of the economy is rising steeply." The Communist Party recognized bureaucratization because they perfected it to an art.

What does state-monopoly capitalism do? It combines state and monopolies into a single power whose sole purpose is to enrich the monopolies, suppress the population, and "launch aggressive wars."[27] The industrial military complex, eager to start new wars around the world, comes to mind.

Some interesting points were made about technology that replaced workers through automation, while displacing small producers. Using bombastic language, the Communist Party stated, "Imperialism is using technical progress chiefly for military purposes." While devouring an ever-increasing fraction of the budget, "The imperialist countries are turning into militarist states run by the army and the police." [28]

The Communist Party conveniently hid the fact that their police state and military readiness kept the Soviet population in a constant state of fear and of need. The communist platform identified the U.S. as the "world gendarme" (police) who at times supported "reactionary dictatorial regimes and decayed monarchies," and at times opposed "democratic, revolutionary changes."

Accusing the "exploiting classes" for "resorting to violence against the people," the Communist Party opportunely hid the mass killings, 100 million innocents who lost their lives to the aggressive communist movement, indoctrination, and power grab.[29]

"Anti-communism is a reflection of the extreme decadence of bourgeois ideology."[30] "Thus any staunch anti-communist born by solid experience with the pathetic life people lived under socialism and communism, by this definition is a decadent bourgeois individual.

The Soviets called the capitalist state the "bourgeois state." It is a "welfare state" for the "magnates of finance capital and state of "suffering and torture for hundreds of millions of working men."[31]

We currently have a welfare state for the masses – almost 50 percent of the labor force today does not work but receives "entitlements" paid by those who choose to work for a living. We also have crony capitalist subsidies and grants for billionaires. Our "free world," said the communist platform of 1961, is a world of "lack of rights, a world where human dignity and national honor are trampled underfoot." [32]

The Soviets would be shocked and disgusted with so many Americans and illegal aliens on the dole. "It is impossible for a man in Communist society not to work, for neither his social consciousness nor public opinion would permit it." According to the Communist Party platform, "Anyone who received any benefits from society without doing his share of work would be a parasite living at the expense of others." [33]

The communist **moral code** included the following principles:

- Devotion to the communist cause
- Conscientious labor for the good of society – "He who does not work, neither shall he eat"
- Public duty and Intolerance of actions harmful to the public interest
- "Collectivism : one for all and all for one"
- Mutual respect and humane relations
- "Honesty, truthfulness, moral purity, modesty and guilessness in social and private life"
- Intolerance of national and racial hatred
- Mutual respect in families and proper upbringing of children
- Intolerance to "injustice, parasitism, dishonesty, and careerism" [34]

The Soviets described **capitalist clericalism** as using the church, political groups, unions, youth, and women's lobby to advance their agendas. Today these groups are used extensively to advance the Communist 2.0 agenda.

The Soviet people with their average equal incomes were never more prosperous than employees of the capitalist economy. What Soviets termed "parasitical classes" under capitalism were no more parasitical than all the communist apparatchiks who stole left and right from the wealth of the people. [35]

Did Soviet communists deliver the promised public consumption funds and goods as promised, according to need and at public expense ? The answer is generally no. When they did deliver some services, they were highly inadequate:[36]

- Caring for disabled people, orphans, and elderly with no family left (few were cared for, were abused, and died shortly in their care)
- Free education (yes, but it was highly competitive and unfairly distributed at the university level)
- Free medical services (yes, substandard care and full of malpractice that was never addressed because it was government run; severe shortages of medicines)
- Rent-free housing, free public transportation (no, it was subsidized)
- Free use of some communal services (yes, libraries, bath houses, culture houses)
- Grants to unmarried mothers (yes, motherhood was rewarded with each new baby born)

The communist experiment at Jamestown, Virginia in 1607 failed miserably when many starved to death. Bonded laborers worked on the communal land but had no incentive to do more because the land did not belong to them. Crops were placed in storage from which everyone took according to their needs but members worked according to their ability. It is human nature that some were more industrious than others and thus worked harder.

Communism did not succeed around the world and will never succeed no matter who is in power because it is premised on a highly organized society of free, socially conscious workers who self-govern and labor for the good of the people. Some men by nature work harder and are more conscientious and altruistic than others. Responsibility, consciousness, industriousness, equality, discipline, and devotion by government fiat cannot be dictated or implemented. Some men or groups of people will always be more equal than others.

Political Class and Crony Capitalism

I was elated but very suspicious when communism failed suddenly in Eastern Europe in 1989. I suspected that the communist elites had decided to go underground to recoup and gain the trust of the west while attempting to rebuild their ranks for a Communism 2.0 re-emergence with a vengeance.

The communists' economic system of surplus was such a dismal failure that it was necessary to hide for a while. People were starving literally and figuratively for capitalism, economic freedom, personal freedom, religious freedom, and a better life for their families. They had reached the breaking point where suffering would change into revolt.

The Romanian military finally turned against their handlers and joined the exploited and long-suffering citizens, deposing the brutal and totalitarian regime with its despised dictator, Nicolae Ceausescu and his wife Elena.

The former communist rulers and underlings scurried like rats, forgetting to destroy all the damning evidence and documents collected over decades of terror, describing the utter depravity of power and abuse against unarmed and defenseless citizens, who were tortured, imprisoned, killed, and their personal possessions, savings, guns, homes, and land confiscated.

Thus began the difficult road to build a free market, a democratically elected government, and to recoup through the justice system the wealth confiscated by the communist goons.

The problem was that those in power were still the former communist elites who had given themselves new titles and affiliations to various parties that were now forming the fragile and corrupt parliamentary democracy.

One former communist party apparatchik after another took the helm of the country. Money borrowed from the west and earmarked for economic development seemed to disappear overnight. The new rulers started amassing vast fortunes and companies with the money and property confiscated from innocent citizens accused of political dissent during the prior communist regime.

The former proletariat, the workers, and we were all workers, benefited in several ways, primarily in the increased standard of living.

1. Thousands of churches were built, Bibles were printed and sold, and religion could be practiced openly again. Many Romanians complained that too many churches were erected, and fewer schools and hospitals.
2. The borders opened to the European Union and a mass exodus of temporary workers commenced. A brain drain of professionals followed, particularly doctors and nurses who were better paid in the west.
3. Food became plentiful - no more bare shelves, endless daily lines, fights over food, and empty markets. Well-stocked supermarkets and malls opened in larger towns.
4. Higher education became more accessible to all and tuition was relatively low. Private institutions of higher learning were founded. When higher education was free, communist party members' children had first choices.

5. Primary and secondary education became globalized, Romanian history forgotten, while students were more and more alienated from their own cultural identity, encouraged and prompted to become "global citizens."
6. The formerly maltreated gypsy population, the Doma people who now call themselves Rroma, migrated back and forth to the EU in search of work and lucrative businesses in the West.
7. People could now afford to take trips and vacations abroad and were allowed to do so.
8. Citizens were no longer watched by the Security Police all the time.
9. The population was free to own guns, to hunt, and to fish.

In spite of some progress, no accountability was put in place immediately because people did not understand democracy, having been ruled by one tyrant after another over the centuries. People were indentured slaves from the moment they were born. Attempts to accountability were met with bribery, select application of the law, and sometimes the lawlessness of the former communist system.

We did not own anything – the communist elites staked their claim to other peoples' homes, land, anything on the farm, chickens, pigs, cows, milk, goats, sheep, vegetables, corn, wheat, eggs, cheese, or whatever a farmer produced.

Citizens welcomed capitalism with open arms – it was a new era they dreamed about from movies they had seen on TV and popular series like Dallas. Things began to privatize and the political class was born from the seeds of the former commies now turned into venture capitalists with other people's confiscated or borrowed money.

Without any vote or referendum, the political class started to dismantle and sell, piece by piece, the aging and non-profitable communist industrial base, factories, steel plants, refineries, oil wells, minerals, coal mines, gold mines, and to cut down forests for timber. The money was pocketed and shared with other politicians who proceeded to build a huge population deception machine – political cabinets and agencies meant to control, much more powerful financially than the previous communist dictatorship.

When the money was spent and the economic crisis ensued, the political class cut salaries 25 percent and pensions 15 percent. The people objected to this forced austerity vehemently, but nobody listened to them. The political class was in trouble and needed more money.

The political class spent the public money, billions and billions of dollars, and all they had to show for were ill-designed infrastructure projects, roads full of potholes, high unemployment, interstates that few people could afford to use, and walking around money for meager briberies for low information voters who were used to the communist nanny state and were unable to think or care for themselves independently. Historical buildings were left to crumble and rust, museums to decay, factories were abandoned, and streets turned into slaloms of pothole avoidance.

The corrupt political class dismantled the old regime and created new institutions, not because the country could not exist or run without them, but because cronies wanted special business treatment, special interests, a special position, or a title they've always dreamed of holding without much education, merit, or effort, and were willing to pay.

Every year the new legislative coalition created new organizations, new structures, new bosses, new state secretaries, undersecretaries, new ministers, mayors, prefects, new institutions, and an ever richer industrial complex.

The former members of the political class never went away, they remained in the system and bloated it, corrupt and without a moral compass, disregarding the law, evading taxes, bribing, and further corrupting the entire political class system.

The economy was always in a state of collapse under communism. The population welcomed "capitalism" with a child-like naiveté and enthusiasm. They woke up eventually when they realized that this capitalism was of the crony variety. The neo-communists and their crony capitalists pushed the theft and corruption to the highest level and limit they could get away with.

Government is now huge, turned into a monster by the political class while the people have watched helplessly, unable to stop its growth and escalation of power. The former commies and the new recruits are now the crony capitalists and the political class.

The few honest politicians get lost in the struggle for power. The political class is composed of parties of liberals, democrats, social democrats, national liberals, communists, laborites, nationalists, and other prominent minorities that dictate policies for the entire country.

Museums and other buildings of historical importance, that had been registered under the ownership of the people and then confiscated by Communist Party apparatchiks and even by the dictator himself, were returned to their rightful owners, and are now private museums or are left to decay, waiting for a buyer to restore them to a former glory.

Two success stories are Bran's Castle near Brasov and Peles Castle in Sinaia. Both museums have been beautifully restored and are open to the general public year round. Peles Castle, located in brown bear country, had been closed for a while during Ceausescu's reign, who used it as his personal residence and playground for his extended family, his children, friends, and visitors they wanted to impress. I remember seeing it as a small child and then, it was closed.

Bran's Castle and the Legend of Count Dracula

We found our way to Bran's Castle via the city of Rasnov. We were surrounded by the majestic Carpathian Mountains, snow topped and covered with forests of blue spruce. The villages, with typical Transylvanian wood and rock homes of the western Romanian province, reminded me of grandma's cabin on the salt mountain in Wallachia, the southern province of Romania. Brown bears often visited our porch, looking for food. Wolves were howling at night, quite close for comfort, their eyes shining in the dark.

The winding roads with hairpin curves offered breathtaking views of different peaks, some rocky with sheer cliffs, and devoid of any vegetation. Dizzying ravines reminded us of what could happen at nightfall if our driving faltered. Rivers were discharging angry waters at the bottom of straight drops. The balmy fall weather with a gentle sun cast golden and green hues of comforting shadows on the picturesque landscape. Waterfalls distant and near thundered and broke the silence, echoing against the rocky cliffs. It was as close to heaven as anyone alive could be.

We parked at the bottom of the ravine and started walking up the steep cobbled road, flanked by old spruce trees. Suddenly, a giant rock revealed one of the castle towers. Built of river rock, stone, brick, and wood, the castle had an irregular shape to fit its narrow location on a crag. The view from the eagle's nest could easily scan miles of terrain on a clear day.

The inspirational castle of Bram Stoker's "Dracula," was strategically located on a rocky bluff, difficult to conquer, tiny by any definition of a castle, and surrounded by stone turrets. The savage nature of the landscape surrounded it with mystique.

Bran Castle tower on its rocky foundation

Bran Castle was built more than 600 years ago. In 1377, King Louis gave the citizens of Brasov the right to raise a fort at Bran at their expense. A citadel was erected by 1382. In early 1400s, the fortress was entrusted to Mircea cel Batrin to help the Wallachian ruler to continue his anti-Ottoman policy. The one and only reference to Vlad Tepes was in 1459 when his troops passed through Bran, attacked and looted Brasov, following the disputes between the Wallachian ruler and the Brasov traders. The castle changed hands several times until 1920 when the town of Brasov donated it to the new sovereigns of the New Romania. Turning the castle from a ruin into a habitable castle, Queen Maria of Romania, with the help of Czech architect Karel Liman, brought water and electricity to the fortress. Three neighboring villages were also connected to the electric plant and the Queen had three telephones installed in the castle and an elevator. Queen Maria turned the old fortress into a genuine royal court. She died at her royal residence at Peles Castle in the town of Sinaia on July 18, 1938.

Peles Castle, the royal residence

In her will, the Queen left Bran Castle to Princess Ileana of Romania. Queen Maria's heart was buried at Bran Castle in a chapel cut in stone. After the forced abdication of King Mihai of Romania in 1947, the communists took over, and the castle became the property of the state and thus a museum. When communism fell in 1989, the royal family requested their properties be returned and, on May 18, 2009, the royal heirs received Bran Castle back. They restored it as Queen Maria's favorite retreat and reopened it as a museum of the never dying citadel.

The inner courtyard is tiny but has room for a well. A rocky, natural beauty is adorned by red geraniums and dark wood railings. The warm ochre painted turrets and a balcony wrap irregularly around the courtyard.

There is a secret passage to the upper floors into the main turret with a 360-degree view. The stairs are winding and narrow, difficult to climb and rather cold. A drafty chill blew and brushed my left side as if a hand was trying to touch my shoulder. I looked over my left several times; I felt an eerie unease. How many have escalated this secret passage and for what purpose?

The Queen's bedroom, study, and other courtly rooms were beautifully restored but very modest by royal standards. The furniture was hand-carved, ornate, solid, and almost ascetic when compared to the opulence in Peles Castle, the royals' main residence. Maria was often pictured on castle grounds in her native costume, handmade blouses and skirts from the local artisans. The cloth, the thread, and the intricate designs were all handcrafted or hand-loomed. The wool in the rugs was spun, hand-dyed, and loomed by locals.

The numerous wooden creaky stairs and the solid, narrow passage carved into the rock have been witnesses to fascinating history for hundreds of years. It was strange stepping back in time, imagining what shadows were lurking in every corner, watching my curious ascent into history.

Queen Maria's bedroom

The irregular shaped inner courtyard of Bran's Castle

Bran

Bram Stoker chose Transylvania, the western province of Romania, as the location of his 1897 gothic novel "Dracula" because of the dark, foreboding feel of the area even when it was bathed in sunshine. The myth of Dracula was so attached to Vlad Tepes and Bran Castle that the locals, when asked about it, shrugged their shoulders with amused looks, and went about their business.

The real Vlad Tepes, the inspiration source for Count Dracula, was known for his strong resistance and valiant battles against the advancement and occupation of the Ottoman Empire. Voievod Vlad was a real hero and founding father to the local population.

Vlad III, Prince of Wallachia (1431-1476), was named posthumously "Vlad the Impaler," for his habit of impaling his enemies and those condemned for capital punishment. Tepes was his Romanian moniker for "Impaler." He ruled mainly from 1456-1462, the incipient period of the Ottoman conquest of the Balkans. Of the house of Draculesti, Vlad III, son of Vlad II Dracul, was born in Sighisoara, Transylavania and died in Bucharest, Wallachia.

Dracula is Romanian for "the son of the Devil." Historians argue over the meaning of the Latin "**draco**" (dragon). Vlad was of the order of the dragon bestowed on his father to defend Christianity. However, the Romanian word for dragon is "**balaur.**" "**Dracul**" is identified in modern parlance as the "**devil.**" The Ambras Castle portrait of Vlad III, c. 1560, is reputedly a copy of an original made during his lifetime.

The Ambras Castle Portrait of Vlad III, c. 1560

Stoker never set foot himself in this "savage" land. Historians described it "barbaric" in earlier third century Roman times when Trajan encountered the resistance of the bearded Dacians.

Trajan's Column in Rome describes in vivid marble relief, the valiant battles between the Romans and the Dacians, which resulted in the colonization of Dacia. The Romans called any foreigner a "barbarus," Latin for "foreign" or "bearded."

Count Dracula is Bram Stoker's bloodthirsty villain who lives perennially cursed as a vampire, condemned across the centuries to a life of darkness in a mysterious coffin.

Vlad III himself used the word Dracula in letters and documents that survive in Romanian museums. Several sources that describe him have obvious elements of bias in their depiction. Romanians saw him as a hero who defended Transylvania from the Turkish hordes and from lawlessness. Russians described him as cruel in his justice and desire for order. The Turks told about the horrors he inflicted on their soldiers during the battles of 1461-62. Germans printed woodcuts of his portrait and of his alleged atrocities. Pamphlets with horror stories such as "The Frightening and Truly Extraordinary Story of a Wild Blood-Drinking Tyrant Called Prince Dracula" were printed in German and found in Nüremberg and other cities, dating from the 1488-1521 period.

Stoker visited London libraries and captured an amazingly accurate description of the surroundings from travel books and friends' accounts. The real Dracula Castle where Bram Stoker positioned his character, Dracula, is located in Tihuta Pass in Bargau Mountains, difficult to access except on foot.

The real Dracula Castle at Poenari is a ruin north of Curtea de Arges with a strategic location to keep the invading Ottoman hordes at bay. Approximately 1,500 steps with metal rails lead up to the walls that formed the former citadel of Vlad Tepes.

Castle Poenari, the real Dracula's Castle

Taking control of the castle was difficult because of its size and strategic location. However, in 1888 a landslide crashed a portion of the castle far into the river below. Foreign visitors were allowed during the communist regime to spend the night inside the remaining ruins, which had been repaired.

Prince Charles, related to the Romanian royal house, walked in May 2003 the 20 km (12.5 miles) between Romania's Putna and Sucevita Monasteries, a popular day-trip, praising the locals for their dedication to traditional lifestyles and heritage.

The local population does not have a choice in their lifestyles. They are very poor, a forced-poverty from the former communist regime that made sure that nobody got ahead of anybody else and everyone survived on a subsistence level, a lifestyle that Prince Charles desires for everybody else. He and his progressive friends would like to establish such a traditional lifestyle across the globe, so long as he and other elites are exempted.

Prince Charles, who took a liking to Romania years ago, loves Transylvania, with its huge bear and wolf population. A nature conservancy advocate, he visited the area often. Promoting his recent visit, he was overheard saying, "Vlad Tepes is my ancestor."

A Stranger in my Own Land

As my husband drove on Republic Boulevard, I was scanning the landscape for sights that looked familiar. After 25 years, everything looked so transformed yet not much different from my childhood years. Newer construction and overgrown trees made everything impossible to recognize, so I thought.

Block A6, Stairwell B of our tenement

As we neared our block A6, I spotted the small shopping complex where we bought our bread, milk, oil, and the occasional sweet treats. Mom sent me many afternoons to buy fresh bread, knowing that I would come back with half of the crust eaten as if some hungry rodent had gnawed the best part. Often I would lose the change which I held tightly in my fist – I was six years old.

My elementary school was obscured by vegetation behind the shopping complex. Most of the private homes in the area had been demolished and the residents forcefully moved into high-rise tenements. This made it harder to identify my formerly familiar surroundings.

I recognized our tenement A6 apartment by the concrete bar that was missing from the bathroom window – it fell in the 1977 earthquake and hung by steel wires like a loose tooth for a couple of years before they cut it off.

I marveled at the 40-foot oak tree, which I had planted in middle school as the red pioneer's volunteer project. The red pioneers were the youth indoctrination brigades of the communist party. The height of the tree dwarfed the five-story building.

The entrance looked the same, the metal rails had a more garish coat of paint, over the many applied over the years. The top of the handrail was still the same yellow plastic. I do not know how this plastic had survived so many years; I used to slide down the banister on it. The window frames were the same; the wall paint design was identical but fresher, and the familiar smells in the stairwell assaulted my senses. The basement was still the dank storage place for potatoes, onions, and rows of jars with pickles and jams.

The entrance door had an electronic lock with a code that only the residents knew. I waited until someone exited and I entered the old building. The metal mailboxes were the same ones that the block informant opened daily in order to spy on my correspondence and write her report to Securitate. I found envelopes opened all the time. She did not even bother to reseal them.

The old banister with yellow plastic covers I used to slide on is still intact, decades later; the ceiling trap door led to the rooftop where we sunburned on the tarred surface, using mom's old blanket. We did not have tanning lotions, oils, and had no idea about the Sun Protection Factor.

Some doors had been replaced by the new occupants. Many remained the same. My former neighbors still lived the truly simple life; it was not by their choice; it took a long time to overcome the limits placed on them by a past communist repressive government. It is still a painful and frustrating journey for some. Freedom is not free and it is difficult to regain once lost for such a long time.

Our apartment door

I did not expect to see anyone I recognized. As I was climbing the stairs, my heart was beating faster not from the effort but the mixed feelings of being there, joy, anxiety, and emotion. On third floor, I rang at number 23 and a mustached man opened the door. It was my childhood friend Emilia's husband. He invited us in while dialing his cell phone to tell his wife. I spoke to her and she recognized my voice immediately. She was in unbelievable shock! My hands were trembling, almost dropping the tiny phone.

The apartment looked very familiar, the same furniture and scent, spotless clean; we girls spent many years playing in this tiny apartment, made even smaller by the presence of my tall husband. He was silently watching everything; he did not understand a word of our conversation but he was witnessing my trembling excitement, trying to read our facial expressions. He insisted that I make this long-overdue journey – I needed closure between past and present.

I met Emilia at our old high school, about ten minute walk from her apartment. She left work to meet us halfway. It felt strange strolling past the cemetery I used to fear every day on my way back from school. It seemed smaller and less threatening. There was now a huge church across the street, a park, and a tiny gas station nestled against the cemetery fence. I wondered which city planner decided that it was a good idea to have a gas station almost in a cemetery. The familiar stray dogs were everywhere, some of them crossing the street at pedestrian crosswalks.

The reunion was incredible, and the time we spent talking, back at her apartment, was not long enough – we had 25 years of catching up to do. Time is such a precious commodity but I thanked God that I was able to find Emilia and rekindle our childhood memories. She is a loving caretaker of her mom who was paralyzed a year and half ago by a stroke. Mrs. C recognized me. Unable to speak, she squeezed my hand with her healthy hand and touched my face. I kissed her cheek and saw the glint of joy in her lively and intelligent eyes. If my trip would have ended then, I knew it would have been worth it. She mothered us with love, care, and whatever food she had for years; I gave her a few moments of joy, remembrance of good times; we were happy in her tiny kitchen, playing and listening to her stories.

Lovely Emilia, my childhood friend, on the left, with two ladies

We climbed to the fifth floor and knocked on the door of apartment 28. My friend Dee's family had lived there. A toothless man answered the door – it was Dee's younger brother, still living there after forty years! It saddened me to see my handsome friend in such a state. I knew it was the result of lack of dental care under the European socialized medicine. I had seen many young and middle-aged people along the way with missing teeth. Rationing of care neglects many people. Fortunately, losing one's teeth is not deadly.

We hugged and took more photos. I glanced at number 30, my old apartment, but did not dare to ring the doorbell. What was I going to say? That I am a stranger who flew 14 hours in a cramped airplane and drove another hour from the airport to see the apartment where I had spent almost twenty years of my life, hunting people who no longer existed but in my memory. Most of them passed away or moved to better places.

As we went down the stairs, we ran into a slim Mrs. Georgescu who recognized me, no longer the waif of years ago when food was scarce and nutrition lacking. Now that food is plentiful, even Romanians are obsessed with weight loss and dieting. To suppress appetite, many smoke.

Once outside, I found the metal bars where we used to beat the dust out of rugs with a wooden paddle since vacuum cleaners were unknown. Between carpet dustings, we used to do gymnastics. I was surprised that the bars were still there after all this time!

The bars for carpet dustings and our occasional gymnastics

> The open market, often empty, where we bought produce, is now bursting with food – plums, apples, grapes, tomatoes, lettuce, veggies, and other fresh produce.

We were unable to visit the old high school; it was off-limits and looked like a bombed out shelter. Workers were completely gutting it out for remodeling. Construction, in line with the planning mismanagement, had started one week before the new school year.

Legal parking was hard to find but then we saw no one giving tickets. The annoying and ever-intrusive police who had controlled every facet of our lives was gone for now.

People were parked everywhere in the neighborhood for lack of space. The roads were so blocked, there was hardly any room to maneuver in between cars on both sides of the narrow streets.

The "green movement" brought out the recycling bins in many cities. A novelty that did not exist before was the public trash bin, even in rural areas. People were slowly becoming more conscientious about keeping their environment and streets clean. Underdeveloped countries are often big polluters of their environment.

I wanted to walk alone, to capture the feelings I missed, or the soul of the place that we all go back to our birth town to rediscover. Whatever I was looking for, was not there, I did not find it. There was a familiarity about the city but life had moved on without me and all I had left now were my memories triggered by sudden smells or sights of something tangible from my youth. I had become a stranger in my own land. Ploiesti was no longer my home; my home was far away, across the Atlantic.

Life in the Village after Communism

Villagers never had an easy life in Eastern Europe. They had to labor for the communist party under ridiculous quotas every season. None of these apparatchiks knew how to run a farm yet they pretended to be experts at everything.

Field production often fell short of the unreasonable expectations and centralized Five-Year Plans; bad weather, floods, unexpected freezes, droughts, and insect invasions added misery to the villagers' tiny share of the crops after **CAP**s (Agricultural Cooperatives of Production) got their share. It was not enough to feed a family.

There were no incentives to try harder when everyone worked for the collective farm and some people worked less than others did but received the same share. How could it be done with one tractor per village and insufficient manual labor, no parts for the tractor, nor mechanics who knew how to repair it?

When forced Marxist cooperatives failed miserably, the communist party stepped in and subsidized the shortfall after punishing local and team leaders.

The land was sold to private investors when communism fell in 1989 and individual villagers reclaimed their land confiscated by the Marxists and started to farm it themselves. Part of the crop was used for personal consumption; the rest was sold on the open market. The work was backbreaking but the villagers kept the fruits of their labor.

Occasionally, an unguarded field of corn was stripped bare of its harvest during the night by thieves working under the cloak of darkness.

My aunt's beautiful vegetable garden near a cornfield.

Life and the standard of living improved quickly with freedom and few regulations. Younger members of many families left the farm and the country to work in the European Union. They returned several times a year with medicine, goods, and money to invest in better farming equipment, a nicer home, a car and other amenities. The grandparents cared for the grandchildren while parents were away.

Villages were connected to the power grid and satellite dishes were visible on the most modest abodes. Cell phones, cars, and access to public transportation, which was provided through generous grants from the European Union, were everywhere.

The concept of taxation was misunderstood in the beginning, but now Romania enjoys a flat tax, which is very easy to calculate, collect, and distribute to various programs.

Gasoline and Diesel were very expensive, $10 per gallon on the average. The steep prices forced most citizens to keep cars in the driveway while using public buses. There were savings in the driving cost because cars were small and all intersections had roundabouts.

A hand water pump left since my childhood.

No running water or indoor plumbing was available unless individuals could afford to install septic tanks. Outhouses were still visible in many yards and so were hand water pumps. It surprised my husband that people could build nice, multi-story homes sometimes with complete bathrooms but no running water.

A neighbor was toiling in her potato field.

Goats in the village

My 77-year old uncle Tache is showing off his bountiful garden.

It was harvest time for many vegetables and fruits, red peppers, green bell pepper, potatoes, corn, grapes, plums, tomatoes, and apples. There was a distinctive smell in the air of wet fertile soil, freshly mowed grass, and natural fertilizer. Nobody used pesticides and the fertilizer came from the many farm animals, goats, cows, chicken, and pigs.

The main transport to the market inside the village, and to and from other villages was the horse pulled wagon, adapted to the asphalted roads with comfortable car tires. These were the Cadillacs of U.N. Agenda 21 transportation platform, no fossil fuels needed.

People were riding bikes everywhere and walking. It was not uncommon to see people in the middle of nowhere between villages, walking for miles to get where they needed to go. We had to be extra careful at night as people wore dark clothing and rode bikes without reflective patches or warning lights.

This cart will be filled to the brim with corn.

A villager is carrying scrap metal to recycling.

Most homes used vines for natural shade and made wine from grapes for personal consumption and for the market. Aunt Nuta, mom's youngest sister, and uncle Tache had a beautiful shaded yard with black grape vines laden with grapes, covering a pergola alongside the house. It was almost harvest time.

My aunt and uncle's harvest of grapes

Villages in general have improved, with new schoolhouses, churches, amenities such as garbage pickup, electricity, technology, small grocery stores, the possibility of more development and growth, but still a poor place left behind on purpose by more than forty years of communist dictatorship, economic exploitation, and dependence on Marxist ideology.

The ruling regime elites served themselves and robbed the country blind initially at gunpoint, while claiming their intent to defend the rights of the proletariat against the bourgeoisie. It was all a lie that enslaved and numbed the population into seething submission for over forty years.

Marxists pretended to pay citizens and the citizens pretended to work. It was not work ethic; it was a symbiotic relationship of poverty and failure, with no incentive for individual creativity and freedom. Fortunately, the Iron Curtain dropped its chains and the population woke up. They never intend to fall prey again.

High School after Communism

The first day of school in 2013

We've never needed protection and guards in U.S. high schools. The community and the local police dealt expeditiously with undesirables and criminal elements. We did not have metal detectors in high school in the 70s or 80s. It is rare now that a school in the U.S. does not have some type of security, including metal detectors. In the old country we did not need security. Everyone was terrified of the police and of the communist party's swift one way ticket to a real jail far away. A communist dictatorship was certainly a strong deterrent to crime in general. Curfews were strictly enforced.

I wanted to revisit the one place that helped shape who I am today and gave me the resolve to move far away to the land of opportunity and freedom – my old high school. I knew most of my former teachers had probably passed away or were very old and long retired. I was looking for evidence in 2012 that the communist indoctrination disappeared. The first positive sign was the change in the name. Gone was the communist era name, C. Dobrogeanu-Gherea – the new high school had been renamed Nikita Stanescu, honoring a famous Romanian poet.

I was surprised to see a guard booth at my old high school and a chicken wire fence. The building had been renovated last year and the concrete exterior painted a happy yellow. After 15 minutes of deliberations, trying to hold on to my professional camera which the toothless guard wanted me to surrender before I could go in, the principal met me at the door for an official tour.

Although it was 5 p.m., classes were still in session and there was a beehive of activity. Students no longer wore the ugly uniforms but casual, age appropriate clothes. A larger gym had been built as an annex to the main school.

The first stop was the faculty lounge. Ten teachers and an orthodox priest were preparing for the next class. A large icon of the Virgin Mary had replaced the "cult of personality" worshipping portrait of the former dictator Ceausescu. The principal introduced me as an alumna. In the ensuing silence, one lady volunteered, she remembered me - we graduated at the same time. As she spoke, a jolt of adrenalin surged. I recognized her voice – it was Dana Malisca, my childhood best friend. For twelve years, we sat in the same classes and the same uncomfortable benches, writing each other notes of boredom whenever we could, and arguing over academic and trivial things constantly. This was beyond serendipity, it was divine intervention. What are the odds that I could find my former friend after so many years during a visit late in the afternoon? I was not so much looking for people, I was looking for a place in time and evidence that the darkness I had experienced was gone. And Dana teaches geography at the same high school!

Dana joined our impromptu tour. The cosmetic changes of the school did not mitigate the feel of unease and inner preservation fear that used to grip me every time I stepped inside the school. The bathrooms smelled strongly of ammonia and I was scared to enter. We used to wade in an inch of urine and water to go to the latrine, a whole in the cement ground with two foot rests. Now they have modern commodes and functioning sinks.

The computer lab had twenty stations of flat screen desktops. It was hot and humid like everywhere else. No air conditioning – the smart meters prevented its use. I was not sure that happened in summer time as well, it was late fall and unusually hot. The students were very welcoming and polite. As soon as I was introduced to them, they quickly started searching my name on the web.

The school added a cheerful biology lab and improved the chemistry and physics labs. Students no longer have access to the locked chemicals, which is a good thing. Dana reminded me how we accidentally set fire to the Christmas tree with the burner from the lab – we had decorated it with so much paper garland, it went up in smoke in no time. Principal Marinescu, whom we all feared, lectured us on fire hazards. He never applied physical punishment to girls who did something unacceptable or violated school standards. Principal Marinescu is 90 years old now and never misses the beginning of the school year ceremony.

I pictured the stage in the courtyard where Dana and I used to get prizes for good grades at the end of each year. We were always in strict competition. The communist party headquarters gave good students a book at the end of the year, sometimes a literary piece, sometimes a propaganda piece. We were not very aware in the beginning as to the content and intent of the gift – we were just happy to be rewarded because we had studied so hard.

We assembled in the same yard every morning for the principal's pep talk of the day and filed into the building one by one through the back door for the usual uniform and matriculation number inspection. We had a number embroidered on our uniforms, indicating the name of the high school that we were attending and the individual numbers that we were assigned. If we ever misbehaved in public, that number was reported to the principal. Because the number was required on our coat sleeves as well, we could be reported even outside of school. If anyone was found dressed inappropriately, he/she was sent home immediately. Shaving, makeup, and inappropriate hair styles were strictly forbidden. Out of wedlock pregnancies resulted in immediate expulsion from school. I did not see any evidence now of nurseries on school premises as is the case in some school districts in the U.S.

Students who had finished their classes were milling about the courtyard casually and relaxed, some talking, some exchanging homework assignments. The gate guard was checking their home passes to make sure, they were not skipping class.

The old gym still had the parallel bars and the beam where we practiced gymnastics. My knees really hurt today from the many falls I had taken off the beam. Sports were not optional and some of us were more gifted than others in gymnastics, handball, volleyball, basketball, and soccer.

Memories are flooding back, people, places, some good, many bad, and ghosts of a terrorized communist indoctrinating past. The school is modern and cheery today, the sunshine flooding through the large windows. A tear found its way to the corner of my eye. Perhaps it is the sun; perhaps it is the repressed memories of pain and discomfort from so long ago. Maybe I am happy that the young faces around me are not subjected to the repressive life I lived.

Students are no longer required to take four hours of home economics. My former teacher, Mrs. Enescu, was not very happy with students like me who hated to sit four hours a week learning how to sew, knit, and cook. If she could only remember me, she is 94 years old and with a keen mind, I would tell her how much her counted cross stitch lessons have helped me deal with stress when I was pursuing my doctoral degree. But I hated cooking!

Women under communism were not encouraged to pursue degrees beyond high school; they were required to be good wives and mothers with a high school diploma. Few places were available for them at the university and men were favored. I've always wondered why liberal women think that communism will install the egalitarian utopia they seek. American women already have more freedom to choose whatever they wish to do than any other culture in the world. Communism would only bring them back to the early 20th century.

Some teachers lamented that, while things have improved tremendously, even adding religion to the curriculum, education has been watered down, de-emphasizing history to make room for the new educational model of the global citizen who no longer identifies with a distinct nationality, with its own language, borders, and culture. The multiculturalism drive from the European Union comes with many grants and scholarships that are hard to turn down. The gym teacher commented in passing that the change was superficially aesthetic and that she hated the highly polished brown doors that looked like coffin lids.

I could not tell the extent of substantive change around my old high school but I was struck by the relaxed atmosphere of both faculty and teachers. Students offered respect to their teachers not out of fear but out of personal admiration for their scholarship. I left the grounds with the satisfactory knowledge that no other generation since 1989 has been indoctrinated into the hideous communist utopia.

However, I was disturbed by the global citizenship drive coming from the European Union with its generous endowments and by the International Baccalaureate program coming from a private company in Switzerland, promoting Gaia stewardship and environmentalism to the detriment of Romanian history, culture, and ethnic traditions.

Socialized Medical Care after Communism

On the morning of September 4, 2011, we landed at Otopeni Airport in Bucharest. I expected the same tired out communist era one-building terminal. I was pleasantly greeted by a brand new, shiny international terminal, built on the model of the German airport in Frankfurt.

The few bathrooms were still smelly with rough toilet tissue that I remembered, some of which still had wood splinters visible in the paper. The unfriendly border guards checked our passports but the scrutiny was brief and we were allowed into the country without a visa!

On the other side awaited my two cousins, our family welcoming committee. The air-conditioned atmosphere on the arrival side gave way to stifling heat on the receiving side, as few Romanians afford to have, cared to have, or use air conditioning. It was 91 degrees and the humidity quite high. We hugged, kissed, and headed for the car rental office, a novelty since I last visited, twenty-five years ago.

For $35 a day, we rented a compact class A Mercedes with an engine that purred like a happy cat. I found out soon enough how expensive Diesel was, almost $10 per gallon, thanks to the heavy European Union taxes and Agenda 21 policy that discourages people to drive their own vehicles and encourages the use of bikes, buses, trains, or walking.

Romanians, who have liberated themselves from communism in 1990, are not going to accept willingly the tenets of Agenda 21. The population will likely be forced or duped into United Nations' control of the population, land use, resources, education, economy in general, and abolishing private property.

We had to be extra careful in villages since bikes were everywhere, goats, cows, and wagons with car tires, pulled by horses. It was anachronistic to see our shiny Mercedes next to goats, cows, and wagons on an asphalted road.

Cars of all makes and sizes were abundant. Parking was very scarce. Infrastructure had not adapted fast enough to the explosion of economic growth, the fastest in the European Union. People parked on sidewalks everywhere. No police in his right mind gave anybody a ticket. In fact, I noticed with glee the scarcity of police, replaced by friendly and rotund rent-a-cops.

Romanians were thin under communism, a sign of poor nutrition. Telling someone that he/she was fat, was actually a compliment because it meant that he/she had plenty to eat. The growing girth of people around us gave an indication that food was plentiful now. Gone were the days when lines for food were winding around blocks. Supermarkets like Kaufland sprung up everywhere.

Traffic police was evident here and there and we escaped a few times being stopped until the 3 a.m. drive to the airport on our return trip home when a young and polite, English speaking cop informed us that the left head light was out and we needed to replace it. He let us go with a warning since the car was rented. Gone were the rudeness, threats, and the arrest that would have occurred 25 years ago, had we been stopped.

We drove directly to the hospital were my uncle had been recuperating since his July brain surgery to remove a hemangioma. I did not know what to expect. I was taking in the landscape of Bucharest as we drove by, a very busy and bustling metropolis by any

European standards but showing the wear and tear of ugly concrete buildings from Ceausescu's communist era.

Stray dogs ("maidanezi") littered the hospital courtyard and the entrance steps, begging for food. The hospital was being repaired and modernized and we had to dodge construction all around us.

My cousin Dragu bribed the guard 5 Euros so that we could go in. Visiting hours were seldom correctly enforced. The guard supplemented his salary with bribes. This was definitely an ugly remnant of communism, which functioned on theft, bribery, and barter. He objected vociferously to my taking a photograph of the hospital entrance as if state secrets were housed therein.

We climbed the stairs to the third floor since the elevator was being repaired, a tired story we used to hear under communism all the time. The more likely explanation was that they were saving on the electric bill. This begged the question, how did they transport patients in and out of the hospital? The interior of the hospital looked more like a hostel with family members caring for the sick and milling about. No nurses or doctors were visible anywhere and it was 11 a.m.

We found the room with two beds, one for my uncle and one for his wife who had been caring for him around the clock for the past two months. She looked tired and haggard and I asked her why she does not go home for a day or two to rest. She said, she could not leave him - nobody would treat him and might kill him through neglect. Hospitals and doctors receive bonuses when beds are emptied early and patients are not "re-admitted" permanently. This brought to my mind the provision in Obama care for death panels. My uncle would certainly have qualified for Death Panels since he is 70 years old.

Uncle Ion was lucky that he had a first-class surgeon who saved his life. Under communism, brain surgery was totally out of the question. He owes his life, however, in equal portion to his wife who made sure that he was medicated properly and cared for afterwards.

It was strange to see an obviously non-sterile hospital room that looked more like a hotel. It was very hot in the room, no air conditioning, and the windows were shut.

The bathroom was down the hall. Uncle Ion was barely able to walk with a cane and with his wife's help. I wondered how she managed when he was entirely bed-ridden.

The bathroom suite for the entire floor had a large sink in which an elderly patient was doing her laundry by hand. A dirty bathtub in the corner looked like it had not been used for years. A second room in this bathroom suite was the janitor's closet with a mop and bucket. A third room was the actual commode with a very large wide-open window, making the commode visible from the above floors. There was no toilet paper in sight and no soap or paper towels to wash and dry your hands.

The new and improved medical system still required that each patient brought his/her own food, towels, toilet paper, linens, pillows and all necessities just like under the old communist system. I was shocked how little progress socialized medicine has made in this regard.

Socialized healthcare is free for some, compensated at 50% of cost for others, particularly when prescriptions are concerned. Doctors are still paid a nominal salary decided by the government and are required to practice in urban or rural areas that the government deems necessary. Dental care is still out of reach as I saw many young, toothless people.

The linoleum floors were dusty and dirty, a patina of respectable dirt, obviously had not been cleaned in a while. How could I explain to my relatives what a hospital looks like in the U.S., the sterile environment, the care, the superior facilities, and the first class medical training?

Another relative, who had pleurisy that required daily antibiotic shots, was hospitalized in an infectious disease hospital for the duration of the shots. Apparently, it was cheaper to keep him on a ward than to pay for the services of a nurse to give him the shots at home. Nurses, as well as doctors, were in chronic shortage. Who wants to go to nursing or medical school for six years and receive the same salary as a person with a high school diploma who performs an unqualified job? When the EU borders opened in 2007, many Romanian doctors and nurses moved to the West for better paying jobs in the medical field.

Several days later, I received a call from my aunt, uncle Ion's doctors wanted to have their pictures taken with me since they had heard that I was an American author. I politely declined. It was refreshing to see that at least those Romanians still respected Americans.

Things have changed but not so much, the socialized medicine and the old, tired mentality still linger. I was looking pensively at this hospital in Bucharest, one of the best in the country. What do the less famous and more rural hospitals looks like? Is this our not so distant future when Obama care kicks in fully? Why are Americans so naïve and willing to trade their exceptional medical care for this sub-standard care? Is it because a charismatic man with no world experience told them that America needs "fundamental change" in the phony "hope" that everyone will be equally miserable and poor, beholden to an all-knowing corrupt government?

A 70-Year Old Unit

Uncle Ion had brain surgery in July 2011 to remove a benign tumor. The fact that this type of surgery was available to him under the former communist socialized medical system was a miracle. The fact that he survived the surgery was another miracle. He was 69 years old at the time.

For two months after he emerged from surgery, he confused past and present, living and deceased, angry with himself that he could not remember important things, words, or recognize loved ones such as his children. He lived in his own confused world while my aunt nursed him back to health.

Although communism has long been gone, the corrupt medical system and the way they operated lingers. Around the clock nursing care was still provided by family members, including food, linens, baths, and expensive meds bought in private or public pharmacies and administered in the hospital. Bribes to medical staff were expected even though salaries have risen from the paltry communist era when everyone was paid equally low salaries.

I visited him in September. It was my first stop after we left the airport. Uncle Ion was happy to see us even though he thought I was my daughter. During the two-hour visit, we noticed the milling about of patients and their families in the hallways, no doctor or nursing staff in sight. His wife was administering medication and his diabetic shots. His son brought him lunch from a nearby restaurant who had been preparing his meals for the last two months, following the prescribed diet.

The only indication that we might be in a hospital was the bed with rails, everything else looked like a cheap motel room with sparse amenities. There was no indication of any sterilization and the common bathroom for the entire floor had no toilet paper, the windows were wide-open for all upper floors to see inside, the tub was filthy, and an elderly lady was doing her laundry by hand in the sink.

We tried to take the tiny 4-person elevator down to the lobby but it was out of order. I wondered how they transported patients up and down the stairs.

Stray dogs were roaming around the hospital courtyard. The gate sentry was happy with his 5-euro mandatory bribe to let us into the hospital. Nobody does anything without a bribe.

Images were flashing in my mind of the luxurious lobby of our American regional hospital, the gift and coffee shops, the spotless and shiny-to-perfection linoleum floors, the professional staff milling about, the comfortable rooms with private, disinfected, and well-stocked bathrooms, the nutritious food prepared with care and served three times a day, and round-the-clock expert care from the medical staff.

Do Americans really understand what socialized medicine provides? Do they really want to have what my Uncle Ion has under socialized medicine? Are they willing to give up the best care in the world they have in America right now? Why? Do they really believe Michael Moore's lies about the "excellent and free" medical care in Cuba? Do they not understand basic economics that nothing is free, somebody has to pay for it? As Margaret Thatcher said, "The problem with socialism is that sooner or later you run out of other people's money."

At some point, rationing of care and drugs kicks in, no matter how old the person is. Even briberies no longer work. The patient has to be placed on a waiting list, prioritized by age.

After a few months of improvement, uncle Ion developed fluid on his brain. All progress reversed. This development required surgery and the placing of a shunt to drain the fluid. He was added to the waiting list for MRI and then another waiting list for surgery. Meantime, his condition worsened. He talked very little and slept constantly.

Ion had become a 70-year old "unit," he was no longer a human being who needed immediate care. Palliatives were his only options after the age of 70 because his worth was deemed small by the medical "death panel."

I suggested more bribes to the doctors and nurses in order to move his name up the list. It seemed to have worked. They moved up his MRI by several weeks. He had successful surgery the following week. His life was in God's hands and the skill of the doctors. We prayed constantly for him and for his medical team.

People used to speak of the golden age, traveling, and enjoying life upon retirement, now it is the fear of being killed by our fellow citizens who have lost their humanity and are dismantling our excellent medical care in the name of insuring more people, particularly those who are here illegally and should be cared for by their own countries.

I do not know of any hospital in the U.S. who refuses emergency care to anybody, regardless of financial status or national origin. It is illegal and unethical to do so. Yet such rhetoric helped pass Obamacare.

I do know doctors who have stopped taking government insurance. Premiums are much higher, deductibles are huge, and co-pays larger. Many full and part-time people have lost their insurance thanks to the Affordable Care Act mandates. I also know that Tricare, medical insurance for our soldiers, who sacrificed so much for our country, has skyrocketed, while civilian government workers who sacrificed nothing for our country continue to benefit from their unchanged stellar insurance.

People are fighting about contraceptives, ignoring the real issues, the loss of control over one's health and body to an omnipotent government that can take all rights away on a moment's notice. If we live long enough, we are all going to become "units" just like uncle Ion.

A Piece of Land and a Moment of Time

In December 1989, communism fell in Eastern Europe and Romanians started the process of reclaiming their land and personal property confiscated by the Communist Party during 1949-1962. My maternal family recently received judicial notification of recovery, 23 years after the suit commenced.

Mom and I were given a plot of land that we have never seen. I am told that it is covered with rocks, the type that an enterprising fellow nearby is already exploiting and selling to construction companies for road building. I am not holding any high hopes or interest right now to plant a crop but it feels strange and empowering at the same time to own an ancestral piece of property that had belonged to my family for generations but was taken by force after World War II. Grandpa would be proud!

In 1921, peasants were given 4 hectares of land. When communists came to power in 1945, under pressure from Moscow, a new agrarian reform was passed, which was meant to disband large farms and to gather votes for the Communist Party. Hundreds of thousands of farmers received small plots of land to grow crops on and feed their families.

Once entrenched, the communist agricultural vision changed. Their leaders were convinced that small properties were not valuable and were condemned to non-modernized operations. At the time, people had plenty to eat and their families were thriving. However, community organizers fanned across the country and convinced them through extensive propaganda that the state would be more efficient in administering the land.

The Marxist-Leninist dogma said, "A small property generates capitalism day by day, minute by minute, spontaneous, and in mass proportions." The small-time farmer feeding his family, with a little surplus, was seen as an individual member of the bourgeoisie, requiring squashing.

The commie's strategy was to turn farmers against the richer farmers through class envy and class warfare, and it worked quite well.

The communists began the process of confiscating land from farmers who owned 50 hectares or more in a violent manner in March 1949 via an immediate executive order or decree. Overnight, farmers were taken out of their homes and forcibly moved to other villages, while their homes, animals, agricultural equipment, and land were seized. Farmers who had some mechanized agricultural tools were labeled "rich and bourgeois." The "socialist transformation of agriculture" that followed was implemented through division of farmers into five categories: those without any land, poor peasants, middle peasants, well-to-do farmers, and the very rich farmers.

The Communist Party introduced the quota system in order to compensate for lack of food in cities across the nation, to make war reparations to the Soviet Union, and to ruin farm operations that were doing well. A significant part of the crops had to be turned over to the state. Oftentimes the farmers were only left with the seed necessary for next year's crop or nothing at all. Thousands of previously well-off farmers or people of modest means were ruined this way, including the very poor whom the communists pretended to protect.

The farmers who opposed collectivization, the joining of small private farms into large, state-owned and controlled farms, were violently repressed through deportations, incarcerations, and confiscation of everything they owned, including clothes.

Deportations involved taking families, who were considered most resistant and uneducable, to labor camps, and placing them in the middle of nowhere, far from civilization and transportation, forcing them to live in a hut in order to have shelter from wind and cold, surviving like the American pioneers in the west. More than 40,000 farmers were deported this way to 18 geographically difficult regions to survive in, the so-called called „special communes" run by the dreaded security police loyal to the Communist Party.

Northern Moldova and Transylvania offered most resistance. The farmers were arrested, shot in their homes, or summarily executed without due process. By 1950, thousands were sent to jail and their wealth confiscated. If allowed to return to their village of birth after a lengthy deportation (1949-1956), farmers found their homes occupied by other families who were staunch communist party members, and were rewarded for their loyalty with ownership of a confiscated home. Injustice was swift and the spreading of wealth was cruel.

Collectivization was completed in 1962 with medal awarding ceremonies. The chaotic and mismanaged agricultural system under communists experienced such a sustained crisis between 1948-1962, that the effects are still felt today, twenty-six years after the communists lost power.

Can this happen in America? Can we lose our land and property to someone else deemed more deserving by constant leftist propaganda? Can we lose our land to wilderness because environmentalists in control force us to move? Or is it already happening peacefully and silently while the population is being soothed with „hope and change," lies and fabrications on a daily basis?

Americans are asleep, ignorant, mesmerized, doped up, or so corrupt that they no longer care what happens to their fellow citizens, their children's future, the future of our country, so long as they have a cushy job, mindless „reality" television shows, sports, a pay check, perhaps bribes, comfortable homes, club memberships, vacations, and most of all, intoxicating power and control.

Redistributing wealth is the only thing communists know how to do brutally and stealthily well. Those who do not pay taxes or hold down jobs protest that it is their right to steal someone else's money. They've even come up with a new euphemism, they are not stealing the wealth of producers, they are merely forcing them to „share the burden. Only liberals on the dole can claim with a straight face that the people paying for their welfare are not „paying their fair share."

But it is stealing! Every moment of time that we must work to earn money and pay taxes that are then spent by our out-of-control government on non-producers is a moment too long that we are slaves to someone else, a moment of time that is stolen from our limited time on earth.

A Late September Day in 2012

Between the suffocating smoke wafting to the third floor of my cousin's villa from burning egg-plants on the indoor grill, the ambulance sirens, the feral dogs roaming the streets all night barking, and the cock-a-doodle of the rooster from the chicken coop across the street announcing the start of a new day, I had no chance to sleep past 7 a.m. The rooster is a bit confused, he cock-a-doodles all hours of the day and night.

I woke up to a cacophony of sounds of a big city, so close to downtown, I could see the cathedral spires from my window and hear the bells toll. The trolley bus running up and down the street below was filled to refuse with humanity packed like sardines, going downtown to work. A mass exodus of villagers occurs every morning and every late afternoon. Driving to work is prohibited by the high price of gasoline, the lack of parking spaces, and the deliberate narrow roads and streets, built at a time when only the ruling elites were allowed or could afford to purchase a car.

I took a picture from the window of my bedroom. The skyline is very crowded by drab high-rises that dwarf my cousin's beautiful and elegant ochre-colored villa. This section of the street has not been demolished yet to make room for more utilitarian concrete twelve story apartment buildings. I love the red roofs on the remaining homes on Malu Rosu Street. They are so cheery in an otherwise landscape of grey and pollution filth. It has not rained all summer long, it is dusty everywhere and grass, unless copiously watered, is brown.

The street is eight-minute walk to downtown, yet many homes still do not have running water - the city never attached them to the water department system. A few have their own electric pumps. Every morning there is a stream of people bringing buckets of dirty water and dumping them directly into the street drain. When the drain clogs and over runs into the street, the fetid smell forces residents to call the city's water department.

I am fascinated by my surroundings yet it is so noisy, I miss my quiet home and the solitude of my woods. Anna's cactus is in full bloom this morning. It started opening last night. The delicate white flower stays open 24 hours and then it dies. I saw it last year when it bloomed earlier. The warmer temperatures this year must have tricked its biological clock and it opened a couple of weeks later.

The hurried urbanites on foot from the surrounding grey and dingy high-rises crowding the landscape discharge into the streets like a huge colony of ants looking for food. True to form, a large portion of the citizens' budget is spent on food and housing. For this reason, politicians like to bribe the lower class voters with tokens of food during campaigning, luring them to the voting booth on Election Day with food as well, including free bus rides.

Not much is illegal in this country anymore, the corruption is endemic. White collar crime or traffic offenses are seldom punishable. Most people know someone who can forgive their violations for the right cash payment or bartering other types of favors. A favor is not just something you do for a close friend or out of kindness, it is commodity money, and must be returned in kind.

Driving on the highly congested roads is a hazard in itself. Drivers never stay in their lanes because they do not exist as a painted space; sometimes one lane is occupied by three cars side by side and only a native can understand the irate hand signals indicating who has the right of way. Passing takes place on the right, on the left, in-between cars, on the shoulder, and on the sidewalk. Pedestrians are fair game even in designated cross-walks. Crowding three cars in a parking space designed for one and double parking are quite common.

Cousin Ana drove us to the abundant market, full of vegetables and fruits, flowers, and busy bees buzzing the nectar oozing from crushed fruits. I bought a purple mum and candles to take to my Dad's grave in Popesti. The gas station attendant filled our SUV with $10 a gallon Diesel. I remained silent on the way to Popesti. Memories were flooding back as landmarks flashed by – the country school where my six cousins graduated from, the creek filled with fish where we bathed in summertime. The road was blacktopped and I was riding in a comfortable car instead of the communist bus smoking oil and fumes inside for two long hours, bumping us with every pot hole.

The cemetery seemed over run with weeds in some places but the view to the valley below was spectacular. I stood on the cliff, peering into the distance, re-living my 5 km walk to the country fair with Grandma and cousin Gigi. The trek seemed endless for five year olds but the reward at the end was worth it – a ride on the merry-go-around, freshly roasted corn, and a clay whistle or toy Grandma always bought us.

Wild flowers bloomed around the dilapidated church, which had fallen into disrepair because there were not enough builders for all the construction projects after the fall of communism in 1989. I had met an architect in Washington State earlier this year who told me that she had traveled to Romania to give pro-bono construction advice in many church projects in Maramures.

Dad's cross has weathered so badly – he passed away 26 years ago, six months before the fall of communism. He would have loved to have seen the positive changes that took place since the demise of Ceausescu's totalitarian regime.

I planted the purple mum and watered it copiously. The owner of a house nearby lent me a shovel and gave me a bucket of water. He was playing with his little girl in the yard. I lit the candles and said a prayer in memory of my Dad's sacrifice. It felt sad and comforting at the same time to be so close to the person who gave me life and freedom, to the places where we grew up, and yet I felt such longing for my home in Virginia.

My heart ached for the unfulfilled past but rejoiced in the present. I was well enough to fly 7,000 miles to place flowers on my Dad's grave and pay my respects to his life cut short by the commies. America, the promised land, has given me so many opportunities that I could not have been permitted under communist Romania. Had I stayed, I would have been just another daughter of the poor and exploited proletariat. Because Dad let me go, I had a shot at a better life. I never squandered this gift.

The water well in front of the cemetery is dry now; people have their own hydro-pumps. The houses nearby are shaded by grapevines laden with golden and red grapes, waiting to be picked. The crop is abundant and the grapes are especially sweet.

I took a few photographs and left my Daddy behind, alone, but surrounded by such simple peace and tranquility. His resting place is sacred ground – he gave his life for what he believed in most ardently, freedom from oppression. I know he is looking over me from heaven because I escaped to freedom and I am able to carry on his legacy. I have touched so many lives in my career, he would be happy and proud of me. His hard work and sacrifice had paid off.

Poplars and Nostalgia

I parked the rented beige Jetta under the tall tree that I had planted as an eight-year old, a life time ago. The entire street was shaded by poplars, painted white half way up the trunk to prevent insect invasions. The lush green trees have grown taller than the five story buildings surrounding them.

On a regular schedule, the Marxist community and street organizers would show up and corral everybody to a day of volunteer work, sweeping the streets, picking up trash, mowing the grass, planting trees, shrubs, pick up garbage, rocks, and pull weeds. Adults would work quietly, fearful of saying something that would be reported downtown, but the kids laughed and ran carefree in their exuberant playfulness.

The hill where I used to run sleds in wintertime was now occupied by 9-story apartment buildings, so clustered together that one could touch a neighbor's hand in the other building through the bedroom window.

Near the stairs leading to another housing project below, there was a patch of heaven where I ran my sled many winters ago, laughing, falling, and rolling in the snow. It was now strangely covered in asphalt on a 30 degree incline.

I walked down trying to retrace my steps but I froze at the bottom of the hill. A large pack of street dogs was approaching, barking and growling. I went uphill quickly, regretful that I could not continue my exploration. The street below, with 40 or so homes still standing, was familiar – three of my school mates lived there with their families. I was surprised that these homes had not been demolished to make room for more high-rise ugly concrete block apartments. Utilizing every inch of space to the max was a primary goal of city planners.

My former home, a tiny match box sized apartment on the fifth floor, still painted the same dirty sea foam green, was oozing decay and pollution stains. Nothing has changed since 1977 when an earthquake damaged many buildings but somehow left ours with cracks and a bathroom window dangling chunks of concrete from the reinforced steel bars, like a loose tooth. That was my family's bathroom window. The concrete bar was still missing and the window looked odd. Why fix it, nobody was going to climb to the fifth floor and invade the home through the gaping hole in the bathroom. The only addition to the old building was a security entry at the main door. All apartments had been bought for $30,000 each by the former communist era tenants who used to pay subsidized rent to the Communist Party. But the prices have skyrocketed since Romania joined the European Union in 2007. Overnight, these shoddy apartments became very expensive property.

The sidewalk was cracked, leading to the shopping center where we bought our milk, bread, bones with meat on them, wilted vegetables, and the few groceries available for which we stood in line a few hours every day. I was shocked that the building had not been demolished to make room for more high rises. Half of it was abandoned in a pitiful state of decay; the other half did not fare much better but it was occupied. A lone, dingy grocery store sold a little bit of everything - the shelves were full of food and merchandise. I don't know why but tears welled up in my eyes. I remembered the empty, clean shelves of my childhood, the pharmacy, the bakery, the dairy, the "cofetaria" selling sweets, the book store, and the pub always full of people who were trying to drown their sorrow in beer and plum brandy. They were long gone. The young shopkeeper ignored me after a cursory look at the middle-aged woman in front of him.

My old elementary school was still behind the shopping center, surrounded by the same fence and locked gates. It was freshly painted a happy yellow. The educationally-themed mosaic created by a commie artist on the left hand side of the building was still intact. It showed mother education as a goddess of communist learning holding a book adorned with a hammer and sickle.

I will never forget the misery and torture the dictator Ceausescu had subjected my people to during his reign of socialist/communist terror. Some individuals have short memories though, especially those who try to excuse the horrible treatment of a nation as a "fatherly," well-intentioned attempt to rid the country of the national debt to the west.

A professor who used to be the communist party secretary to the university system during Nicolae Ceausescu tried recently to blame Ceausescu's demise on his announcement in 1989 that Romania had paid off all its debts to the west; additionally, Ceausescu allegedly forbade the Romanian government to seek any foreign credit. In other words, Romania had become such a threat to the one world government bankers and their ill-gotten interest-based fortunes that they were able to get rid of Ceausescu and "punish him physically for his insolence." Perhaps this professor forgot that Ceausescu did not consult the Romanian people if they were willing to suffer so much hunger, cold, poverty, neglect, misery, torture so that Romania would owe no money to the west. He also forgot the brutal abuse, imprisonment, and swift punishment citizens suffered if they dared to criticize the communist party.

This professor's national debt explanation makes for an interesting conspiratorial theory. The powerful western bankers cowed by a "maverick" defiant dictator who stood in their way to control the world financially. God forbid Ceausescu's move would be copied by other dictators and turn into a contagion around the globe, robbing the bankers of their fortunes acquired by shameless interest charged to poor countries. Did someone force his hand to sign on the dotted line? Did the dictator with an elementary school education not become a wealthy billionaire from these loans, and lived a life of luxury while his people starved? Did I miss something here?

Communism did not die behind the Iron Curtain in 1989 – it re-emerged in a more nefarious form around the globe, promoted by the compliant media and hypocritical Hollywood. McCarthy was right about some of them after all.

The has-beens of the old communism and total government control are nostalgic for the good ole days of totalitarianism, romanticizing the past, trying to reclaim their positions of power and privilege. The global communism of U.N. Agenda 21 is making great stride, using environmentalism, land preservation, zoning, and care for the planet as a tool. And the Fabian socialists in the west are winning the hearts and minds of low information voters who believe anything they are told over and over by the main stream media. If a lie is repeated often enough, people start to believe it's the truth.

Back to Our Future

On a hot and steamy October day I entered my aunt's yard with caution. I had parked in the road since few people had room for a garage. The rusted gate creaked loudly. Two scrawny cats were playing in the tall weeds by the runoff ditch. I could hear hens cackling in the back yard and the occasional grunt of the pig. A mild wind was blowing and the fetid smell of farm animals mixed with outhouse odor hit me as soon as I stepped inside.

The natural grapevine pergola stretching over the yard from the house roof to the tall fence offered some shade in the scorching heat. The grape vines, turning yellow by now, had been picked of grapes. Nobody was in sight. I could see the vegetable garden in the distance. A tall pile of freshly dug potatoes and ruby red bell peppers on the grass served as playground for a tabby kitten.

I knocked on the front door. Stefan, my cousin's eighteen-year old son, hopped to the door on crutches. In spite of the pain and misery, a big smile lit up his face. He had split his big toe open with an errant ax which had flown out of his inexperienced young hands. He had tried to help his grandfather cut wood for winter. Bleeding profusely, he was transported by bus to the nearest emergency room in town, about five miles away to the county hospital.

Stefan had been in a cast for six weeks and was anxiously awaiting the moment to have it removed. I promised to take him to the emergency room by car instead of the usual bus. The county hospital had not changed from the hospital I knew in the seventies. It looked just as dingy, dirty, and poorly lit. The low wattage CFL bulbs cast an eerily glow that gave me a headache. The paint was chipping everywhere, there were suspect stains on the linoleum floor which had seen better days and the walls were soiled by filth and bloody emergencies. The littered yard was occupied by several stray and mangy dogs.

After waiting hours in the crowded and sweltering hospital, Stefan was seen by a gruff doctor whose demeanor was less than friendly. The emergency room doctor called in a nurse to help him cut the cast. From the cloud of white dust, Stefan's toe emerged. It was swollen, twisted, and the inexperienced stitching looked like the patchwork of Frankenstein's monster. The doctor dismissed Stefan, telling him to stay off the foot for two more weeks and to walk on his heel. No advice to assist him cope with the swelling, no therapy, no boot to help him walk for two weeks, nothing. I was shocked! I tried to ask questions, the doctor looked at me dismissively, and walked out of the room.

Proper care and treatment according to the Hippocratic Oath is costly. Medical care is free but it is only given properly if bribes are offered to doctors and nurses – walking around money, they call it. Stefan's mom is relatively poor like most Romanians who are still struggling to overcome forty years of communist oppression.

Digi24, an online Romanian magazine, publishes photos sent by patients of nightmarish hospitals around the country where the smell, the rusty beds, the incredible filth, the bugs, and the putrid stench drive patients away to private clinics - if they can afford it. Having received millions of euros to modernize, these public hospitals operate by asking patients to buy their own sheets, towels, and meds, just like during the communist era of socialized medicine. In a Constanta county hospital, the head of oncology is alleged to have sought cancer treatment in the U.S. Babies and children hospitalized in the pediatrics section have died from simple colds.

Private medical insurance is available but it is not cheap. By law, every Romanian has medical insurance, seven percent of their salaries, payable to the government. This insurance only covers part of the medical care and drugs. Every company also pays a percentage to the government for each employee and must have a contract with a medical clinic for yearly checkups. Taking into account the current sorry state of hospitals, the government does not seem to be a very good, wise, and honest steward of the money collected. The bureaucrats, ever in need of more money, want to institute a hospital stay fee per day, per patient, in order to raise more funds. And then, there is the mandatory individual medical card for everyone with a microchip that contains medical information for all individuals, including automatic consent for organ donation after death. Is this scheme one way to fund more medical waste and will medicine be interested in keeping a patient alive?

Medical care was given properly to the elites when the few, self-appointed apparatchiks, ran the communist country. If the masses wanted the same, they had to pay in a stuffed white envelope. I remember my Dad's doctor. When he opened his office drawer to retrieve my Dad's 5,000 lei bribe, cousin Mariana saw rows of envelopes with the patient's name neatly written. My Dad had died and Dr. Arsene was returning the money at the request of the family. After all, he did not help Dad survive and burials were expensive.

Twenty-six years ago when my Dad passed away in Romania, communist medicine functioned on bribes and favored the elites in power. Omnipotent communists received proper care and the best medical treatment available at the time in hospitals built just for them. Men like my Dad, who had no love, nor allegiance for the communist elites, had to go home to die or to a dingy hospital ward.

Socialized medicine in Romania today, although dictated by the European Union standards, has not changed that much. They have perhaps better equipment, a few newly built private clinics and hospitals, and better training. But bribery in public medical facilities or care in private clinics are still the way to receive proper and timely health care.

How is an eighteen-year old supposed to walk to school on his heel for two weeks in order to protect his grossly swollen, incorrectly stitched, and improperly healed big toe?

From Communist Economy to Market Capitalism

Transitioning from a communist/socialist controlled economy to a mixture of capitalism and European socialism was not painless for the former communist Romania. After the bloody revolution of December 1989, the country embarked on a series of difficult economic changes and adaptations that culminated in its admission into the European Union on January 1, 2007.

Jumping from the communist party's inadequate and random five-year economic plans that bore no resemblance to the needs and wants of society to a market system based on supply and demand was quite difficult. Between 1948 and 1989, Romania had a state-controlled economy built around the heavy industry.

Today, one third of the labor force is involved in agriculture but produces only 10% of Gross Domestic Product. Another third of the labor force works in industry and produces one third of GDP. The rest are involved in the service industry.

Lacking sufficient supply of minerals and other resources, Romania imports raw materials and fuels, which it refines. It has been an important oil-producing country in the past. Italy, Germany, France, and Turkey are its largest trading partners.

Ceausescu's failed economic policies, the failed attempts to privatize the economy in the 1990s, endemic corruption that ruined the industry and reduced GDP by 50 percent, put Romania into a poor country category in the 1990s.

Romania did not owe much money to the west when the communist president Ceausescu was forced to resign. The megalomaniacal dictator misspent the country into bankruptcy by investing unwisely in heavy industry and building monuments and a huge palace "of the republic" to himself and his greedy wife. It did not matter to him that Romanians had more prescient needs for daily survival. No historical monuments or old churches stood in the way of his hideous palace. They were all demolished to make way for his grandiose masterpiece.

Free to worship, citizens are now rebuilding churches, 6,000 and counting. This beautiful cathedral was built in my old neighborhood in Ploiesti.

Millions of dollars were borrowed after Ceausescu's demise by unscrupulous individuals from the former communist regime who never paid back their loans, had no intentions to pay them back, causing the collapse of many banks in the process, and necessitating bailouts similar to our TARP. Those who were honest then and refused the loans, are still poor today.

Former regime leaders, politicians, and their families bought companies and other personal investments with the borrowed money. Some also sold piece by piece, for personal gain, various state-owned factories to foreign investors without any scrutiny or challenge from the complicit legal system. The corruption was endemic and the population at large could do nothing about it.

Romania's economic growth was among the fastest in Europe at 8.4% in 2008 and three times the EU average.

The global financial downturn affected Romania heavily when Gross Domestic Product contracted 7.2% in 2009, forcing the government to enact austerity measures and to borrow heavily from the International Monetary Fund, while carrying a budget deficit of 6.6 percent.

People's lives in general have improved. Many main roads have been enlarged and some country roads paved. Most villages were electrified. Small private companies sprouted like mushrooms in both urban and rural areas. All villages now have grocery stores, phone service, satellite dishes, a new schoolhouse, and a new or remodeled church. Bikes are everywhere, encouraged by grants from United Nations' Agenda 21 European groups.

Grocery store in my childhood village, Tirgsorul Vechi.

Fancy bike path in downtown Brasov

There is an explosion of automobiles, even in the country, but fuel is very expensive, $10 or more per gallon. Evidence of UN Agenda 21 measures is everywhere: new high-rise tenements with shops on the first floor, smart meters, lack of parking but an abundance of bikes, walking, and public transportation, anemic use of electricity which is very expensive, air conditioning units that are seldom used because electricity is cut off for several hours a day if consumption peaks. People were also brain washed into believing that A/C is damaging to lung health.

Cars and goats sharing the road in my Grandma's village.

Gas stations have been placed in the most unexpected locations like the middle of a cornfield or a cemetery. There was one station built on the sidewalk that I used when I went to high school, crowded against the cemetery wall.

Parking spaces are so few, people park on sidewalks or block the lanes closer to the curb. No cops in sight were giving tickets.

People are free to travel, free to move from town to town, but are still bound by the communist era union labor I.D., a passport sized book that holds the official employment history and stamped record of every citizen.

Having joined the European Union in 2007, the socialist nanny state was reintroduced through a novel idea, welfare. There were no more lines for food or basic goods as we experienced under communism, but I photographed a line and curiously asked what they were selling there. A strapping young man answered, perhaps embarrassed or puzzled by such a question, that they were standing in line for social welfare. All of a sudden, when easy money was being offered, an unusual number of people had become needy and extremely poor.

Social welfare line

Older people who did not like the competition of a free market, became nostalgic for the old communist regime, some putting flowers on Ceausescu's tomb, although nobody knew for sure whether he was buried there. They preferred the certainty of poverty under communism to the uncertainty of capitalist competition. The

PSD, the Social Democrat Party, in collusion with European Socialist Party seized on this opportunity to buy their votes through occasional gifts of food and money.

"Together in Europe"

"The Left Makes Romania Straight Again"

Brigitte Bardot, an aging French actress, came into Romania and introduced PETA to mass consciousness. The citizens understood her message and expensive campaign that they were to leave dogs and cats alone to roam the streets and free to reproduce to the point that they became a huge problem for every village and town. They are everywhere, neglected, some fed, some hungry, diseased, and pitiful. They've even created a word for them, "maidanezi." Attacks on humans and particularly on children have escalated, sometimes resulting in death.

My cousin Mircea, the ever loving and generous human being that he is, fed twenty strays at his business, and quite a large contingent of mutts became sheep dogs on his farm in Valea Dulce.

This stray dog made his home around the museum entrance in Sinaia, Castelul Peles.

There are supermarkets everywhere, people have plenty of food, seem happier, look healthier, and smile more. Food is being imported because some fields are no longer worked, they have been abandoned when the communist co-operatives were closed and the land sold to investors.

Some fields are idle because it is too expensive or too hard to put in crops. Young men and women who were providing the labor have gone to other countries to make decent wages in Spain, Italy, France, and Germany. They come back a few times a year to see their families, build new homes, buy a new car, appliances, and provide much needed cash.

Private medical clinics and hospitals were built but few Romanians can afford to use them. Socialized state run medical care is the same communist style care with newer testing equipment such as CT scans and MRIs. People have to wait months and years for their turn to use the new equipment and tests that we take for granted and we can schedule in a few days, not months.

Drugs are now available but even the socialized medical system only gives free drugs to fewer citizens, the rest have to pay 50 percent of the cost. Pharmacy shelves are no longer empty as they were under communism.

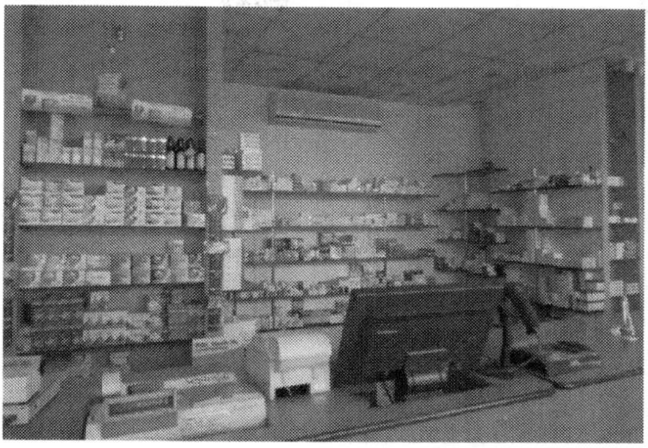

A modern pharmacy in my hometown of Ploiesti

Hospitals operate the same way they used to under communism, patients have to be cared for pre- and post-operative by a family member; sheets, food, and all necessities, including drugs must be purchased by the patient.

Doctors do not have a say in their salaries and must go to the town or village they are assigned after graduation and practice medicine. There is a chronic shortage of nurses and doctors because nobody wants to study six years in college in order to make the same salary as a high school graduate. Bribes are still given, expected, and accepted for better service.

Education has gone down in quality. Students are discouraged from studying history and no longer take pride in who they are and where they have come from. It is a deliberate attempt to indoctrinate the new generation into the European mindset of a one world government without borders, national identity, and sovereignty.

Communist era uniforms are gone except for kindergarten and elementary school. Other students wear western clothes to class. Girls parade in more revealing attire than necessary while boys dress age appropriate. The young are being targeted through clever advertising campaigns by local socialists with copious help and funds from the European Socialist Party, which has infiltrated the cities.

The Social Democrat Youth Party poster

Historical buildings are abandoned and uncared for, rusting and decaying in the wind, rain, and snow. Graffiti covers the walls of these monuments, of historical and public buildings, and nobody seems to care.

Abandoned historical building covered in weeds; it is where communists officiated weddings for the record. I got married here first then in an Orthodox Church.

Cheating on exams is endemic, many students pass major exams by buying the tests from their professors. Scandals are covered in the press.

Food is plentiful but expensive. Prices mirror European Union levels but salaries and pensions have not caught up to the same level as the European Union (EU), on the contrary, they were cut to meet the president's established austerity measures as dictated by the EU.

Housing prices are over inflated when compared with similar housing in Europe. Expensive boutiques cater to the very rich while ordinary citizens buy cheap imports from China.

Villagers who chose to keep their parcel of land grow their own vegetables, corn, wheat, barley; some raise a pig, a cow for milk and cheese, a few goats, sheep, chicken, rabbits, and ducks. In a food shortage situation, farmers will fare much better than urban dwellers.

Time will tell if Romania will continue its development on the path of free market capitalism or will be forced to adopt the European socialist nanny state model entirely, in essence returning to its painful communist past.

What Communism Wrought

On March 28 my Dad would have been 86 years old. I still mourn his tragic and premature death at the hands of communist goons who took over the country of my birth and terrorized people for 41 years. Dad was barely 61 and healthy.

The benevolent dictator Ceausescu ruled Romania with an iron fist, lording over the frightened and defenseless population. His portrait was everywhere next to his hideous wife, "the Mother of the Country." She had given herself that title along with a Ph.D. in chemistry. A fifth grade dropout, she had grandiose ideas of her faux accomplishments.

Dad hated Nicolae Ceausescu and his co-dictator wife, Elena, with a passion. He never hid his utter disdain for the arrogant, narcissistic, and uneducated couple who rose from the poverty of community organizing with empty promises of paternal and maternal care for the weak, the poor, and the downtrodden, to a life-style of the rich and famous.

Torturing, imprisoning, and killing millions of innocents, the Ceausescus had appropriated their possessions and amassed such a vast wealth, it was hard to tell how much money he had in Swiss bank accounts, how many art pieces, jewels, land, and homes.

The dictator was proud that he gave "homes" to all his subjects, the proletariat, crowding country and city folk alike into high-rise concrete apartment blocks, while taking their homes and land for agricultural cooperatives or grandiose buildings and palaces dedicated to the Communist Party. Hastily built of reinforced concrete, the nine to twelve story apartments were Spartan, ugly, cold, dirty from the heavy pollution, and chipping concrete chunks like loose teeth.

The benevolent dictator made sure that there was no middle class left when he finished his fundamental transformation of the former prosperous monarchy into a socialist/communist republic. He kept changing his mind as to whether the country was a socialist popular republic or a communist one, frequently altering the Constitution on a whim, adding more articles, while robbing Romanians of their clearly stated rights and freedoms.

People were frightened to speak to their neighbors or relatives because nobody knew who was an informer. The country had become a country of snitches for a few extra lei (the official currency) a month, meat and other necessities, proper medical treatment at the Communist Party polyclinics and hospitals, and access to drugs at their well-stocked pharmacies. Adults turned in their own parents and relatives. Children often did the same, without realizing that such childish indiscretions would send their parents to jail.

Dad was under the commies' radar all the time because he refused to be a member of their party and always blamed them publicly for destroying the country. He was not shy to assign blame and to criticize the dear leader and his wife. Although a pacifist who could not hurt a fly, Dad was always beaten and imprisoned every time the Ceausescus traveled anywhere near my dad's location.

The peoples' discontent and misery was palpable but they did not dare discuss their thoughts with anybody. Dad had the courage and foolishness to say what was on his mind. He did not care that the communists had built a very strong police state: regular police, traffic police, security police, economic police, military police, and ideology police. Dad really believed in human beings' inalienable right to freedom and economic independence, not dependence on an omnipotent government. He saw every day how this all-powerful government robbed people and gave back very little, while pretending to care.

Since goods were in such short supply due to poor centralized planning by communist bureaucrats, people learned to survive through stealing from work and bartering. Dad hated theft and reported the culprits all the time. Since theft at work started at the top and trickled down to the lowest ranks, orders were often given to punish my dad for daring to expose the thievery. He was beaten many times for his honesty. He always recovered, more resolute that he was doing the right thing.

One day his luck ran out. A savage beating and dropping from a refinery scaffold into a metal shaving pit resulted into a cracked skull that was not x-rayed or treated at all at the state-run hospital. Receiving little food or water, he died four weeks later, a slow and agonizing death, shrinking to half his healthy size.

Dad is in Heaven now, gratified that his premature death was not in vain. Many people who know and understand how totalitarian regimes rob humans of their freedoms and their God-given rights, are picking up the opposition against communist utopia and its "social justice" and "equality" propaganda

.

Being Bourgeois

Ana and I picked up nine-year old Stefan from school one October day, a gorgeous Indian summer day before the winter chill. A musical prodigy, little Stefan is a genius with a penchant for Italian food. Half a block from his art school is a restaurant called Da Vinci's, always bustling with patrons dining under the grape vine pergola.

I was happy to see so many people out to lunch, able to afford food and particularly restaurant food, previously considered a luxury under communism that only the ruling elite could afford and felt entitled to have and enjoy.

Adjacent to Da Vinci's was an old stately mansion in a terrible state of disrepair. A tall fence covered in vines obscured the full view to the house. I peered through the wooden slats that had separated here and there where the nails broke or the wood decayed. The gate opened with a groan and I stepped inside the yard. Someone forgot to lock the gate. There was neither a trespassing warning nor any sign of habitation. The formerly tended front garden was overcome with tall weeds, growing from the most unlikely places – like the many cracks of the cement garden path.

I walked to the front door and rang the massive lion head door knocker. It made a hollow sound. I waited for a few minutes but nobody answered. I looked through a window – the house was empty and had been empty for quite some time.

The mansion was oozing rust from everywhere but especially the wrought iron front foyer bump-out. The stained glass windows were still beautiful, just as I remembered them. I used to count the squares and name the colors to pass the time. The walls were cracked and peeling and the fancy silk wall paper hung desolate onto the floor stained from water leaks. The Bohemian crystal chandelier was still hanging in the dining room, missing bulbs and electricity. The heavy rosewood furniture with strange carvings was gone. The parquet discolorations bore witness to the place where they stood. Did the owners remove them? Were they sold at auction? Did the communists apparatchiks confiscate them in the 1980s and moved them to their villas?

Aunt Ecaterina's bedroom bay window that I admired was missing the heavy curtains. Mom used to open them to let fresh air in. Miraculously the dingy glass was not broken. I sat on a pillow in the bay window many Sundays checking out the lush rose garden, now a jungle mess of weeds, or staring mesmerized at the rain. Mom and aunt Ecaterina talked in hushed tones and she cried a lot.

She always wore her finest housecoat and slippers made of rich silk brocade. I did not understand at the time what secrets they shared, why we had to walk so much to her home every weekend. It was a trek I dreaded but I was not old enough to stay home alone.

Her husband had been arrested because he was bourgeois. It must have been a terrible crime, I thought at the time. I asked Grandma several times why her youngest brother was in prison but she always avoided my question and turned her eyes away, waving her hand in the air.

Years later I understood. Grandma's brother had acquired too much land and a nice home and that was a crime in the new communist regime. He had worked very hard to build a successful store from scratch, built the mansion, bought some land, got married, and had a son whom he sent to the best schools to become a lawyer.

Class envy and re-distribution of wealth sent him to prison for seven years. His wife was devastated! The communist regime confiscated all the land, the store, the bank accounts, and the furnishings. They left Ecaterina's ornate bed. She became so depressed; she seldom got out of her matrimonial bed. Mom tried to cheer her up with our weekend visits. I only looked forward to her sour cherry preserves on rye bread. It was a real treat.

Nobody knows how uncle Pavel survived seven years in jail – it certainly was not a walk in the park being beaten daily and eating potato soup and bread. He died several years after having served the full sentence. Aunt Ecaterina never recovered from her depression. Not only did she have to suffer the indignity of losing everything, including the love and comfort of her husband, the communist party moved two families of strangers into her home. Nine more people made the large house look suddenly small and crowded. She had to share the kitchen, the hallways, and bathrooms with total strangers. She lived long enough to see her only adult son succumb to lung cancer. I wondered if the grandchildren inherited the mansion and perhaps did not have the money to remodel such a huge home.

It was bittersweet, stepping back in time almost five decades, remembering the misery and abuse of communism. I walked back into the street and to the restaurant. By now, Ana and Stefan had arrived and were looking for me. I glanced back one more time at the rusty tin roof – the sun was shining but the house looked forlorn and leaning.

I smiled when Stefan gave me a hug and threw his back pack on the ground. The day was going to be all right, the fog of the past dissipated. Unpleasant memories still hound me, triggered by unusual circumstances. I went back to Romania to revisit my past but the unplanned encounters with the ghosts of communism were still painful.

Volunteer-Forced Student Labor

As we loaded the bus, there was standing room only. There were no seats on the open truck, just sides to protect the cargo from toppling over. The only reason we didn't fall over is that we were packed like sardines. When the moving truck hit a pothole, and there were many of those along the way, the entire mass of humanity swayed back and forth, leaning a lot of weight on each other and squashing momentarily those along the edges. There was nothing to hang on to, so we clung to each other for dear life. The dust swirled around, chocking us, mixed in with the Diesel exhaust fumes. Once we left the city, nothing was paved. We were only going about 9 miles, however, under those conditions, it felt like 90 miles.

We tried to keep a cheery disposition; we tried to think of it as an impromptu field trip, getting away from the drudgery of daily communist indoctrination and rigorous classroom work. At least we were outdoors in the sun, dust, and heat, not stuck behind an uncomfortable wooden bench in the classroom.

We were going to pick grapes in the hills of the nearby cooperative farms, a misnomer of sorts. There was no co-operation at all. The laborers were supposed to own the farm collectively, but the land had been confiscated from small farmers, who were quite successful in their operations, and the communist party received the majority of the crop; the remainder was divided evenly among the many villagers who actually put in the back-breaking work every day for the entire season. It was barely enough to justify their existence. And the free labor from students each fall and spring was an added bonus to the communist party. They subtracted the amount of labor from what was owed to the villagers.

We arrived at the sprawling vineyard. We were instructed how to cut the grapes off the vines. We were told that unless we brought our own food and water, there would not be breaks to eat or drink. We thought about eating grapes but they were sprayed with a whitish chemical to keep pests and disease from destroying the harvest. After an entire day of starvation and thirst, I found an old glass bottle, filled it with water and fixed a piece of bread with a slice of Parizer, a fatty type of cold cuts. Back then there were no disposable water bottles, sodas, or coolers. Ice was unheard of for the masses. Thermoses were way too expensive for ordinary people, the proletariat – it was a month's rent. The elites rolled in money, food, and luxury but the rest of the people suffered.

My relatives no longer live this way in Romania since communism was rejected by the 1989 revolution. But there are still people around the world existing under some form of religious tyranny, dictatorship, or communism.

The youth today seem to be mesmerized by empty communist rhetoric, indoctrination, and social justice/equality promises by deceptive elitist governments and environmental groups who claim doom and gloom, planetary destruction unless we save ourselves from the man-made global warming/climate change.

Cuba still sends school children today to pick crops for two months out of the year. It is forced and abusive labor. There is nothing "volunteer" about it. The American naïve fools, who repeat that education in Cuba is free, have not seen the student slaves who pick or put in the crops so that Castro, his family, and the elite commies can stash away billions in Swiss banks. Older students are forced to pave roads or work in construction. Without this "volunteer" work, students could not attend the university.

Sure, American students volunteer for community service in their respective schools, but they do it because they want to make a difference, they are not forced to do so, away from their families and with little food and water. And now, we are going to copy Castro's shameful model of uncivilized society because low information young Americans have voted for the fundamental change of our society, including our stellar healthcare. With millions of unemployed Americans, the highest number of welfare recipients in history, and the national debt galloping to its $19 trillion point of no return, how is that working out so far?

Blue Jeans Like John Wayne's

When my future fiancé asked me what I wanted for my 18th birthday, I did not hesitate - a pair of American made blue jeans.

I was watching John Wayne westerns to improve my English skills and the cowboys, at least the celluloid ones from Hollywood, sported well-worn and seemingly indestructible Levis covered with chaps.

Blue jeans had become a status symbol of sorts in the poor Iron Curtain countries. It was not for the same reason Americans loved clothing fads – to prove that they were rich, trendy, and fashionable. We liked jeans because they represented freedom, exploration, and the ability to cross unchartered borders and territories. Jeans epitomized a physical freedom that we longed to have but were only allowed in spirit because, to our communist rulers, everything western was decadent and dangerously capitalist. Profit and capitalism were dirty words.

To make durable capitalist jeans inaccessible to the masses, no importation was endorsed. Black market dealers made huge profits by selling cheap knock-off denim pants smuggled into the country from Turkey and sold for $150 a pair back in 1977! Most people earned $70-80 a month, including specialized doctors. Stories were told of foreign visitors, approached by locals in the street, wanting to purchase the jeans they were wearing.

I was so excited that I would finally own a pair of denim pants, but not just any pair, blue jeans made in America, indigo blue denim with rivets, snaps, a metal zipper, and the famous Levi leather patch.

My birthday present arrived two weeks late. As usual under communism, the package was received at the post office downtown and the security police inspected its contents before I was allowed to pick it up. It took an hour to walk downtown but I did not mind this time. They opened the box and, to my surprise, it contained a vest and a matching skirt made of blue dyed soft material with a denim-like pattern. My elation deflated like a huge balloon.

My fiancé's mother, a very caring and proper southern lady, thought blue jeans to be an inelegant 18th birthday gift for a young lady and took it upon herself to find material, a suitable pattern at Hancock Fabrics, and an enterprising seamstress willing to sew, subject-unseen, the matching vest and skirt in record time for $10. I knew the price because "rotten capitalists" had to declare the value of any gift package sent to communist citizens. The commies then assessed 40 percent custom duties. After a thorough examination of the contents to make sure that there were no subversive materials hidden, I took possession of my package and paid the equivalent $4, exchanged times 12 into the pegged Romanian currency, the worthless "leu."

There is a very good reason why I cringe every time the TSA goons rifle through my belongings at the airport and frisk me. We were subjected to many unwanted bodily and purse checks during my almost twenty years of life under communism, including upon exiting department stores. It was always assumed that we were criminals engaged in stealing from the oppressing government that was actually robbing the country blind.

Always grateful for my gift, I took pictures with the unusual outfit on, sent it to my future mother-in-law and wore it a few times before it faded. My heart was still longing for a real pair of jeans.

On my 21st birthday, very pregnant with my first daughter, I went shopping with my friend June D. She was buying clothes in an old fashioned mom and pop store in our small southern town. I had told her the story of my 18th birthday blue jeans that remained just a dream. It must have struck a chord with her. When we finished, she dropped me off to my home and handed me a beautifully wrapped box. Inside was a brand new pair of indigo blue Wrangler jeans. I was very pregnant and unable to wear them yet but I was jumping with joy, on the inside. The price tag was mistakenly left inside: $20.

Every year since that time, I never forget to pay it forward. I have given away my expertise, translation services, food, toys, books, shoes, and clothes, especially blue jeans, to other legal immigrants like me. In my mind, jeans were the quintessential expression of the American pioneer spirit and of boundless personal freedom.

Wormy Banana

My 80-year old mom is sitting at the kitchen table dissecting a banana as if it was a biology specimen under a microscope. I watch her for a few minutes intently before I ask her what she is doing. With a scientific look of Eureka discovery on her face, she tells me, she is looking for worms. Worms? She is 100 percent sure; the bananas I just bought at the grocery store have worms, especially since they had ripened enough to be extra sweet and mushy. She is peeling away and separating the banana core into smaller segments, believing that the tiny white fibers are worms.

I started to explain that they do not, but I stopped short. Mom spent most of her adult life in the Eastern European block where fruit flies were rampant and uncontrollable. Insecticides such as DDT, although banned in this country, were used on most crops and vegetables low to the ground, but it was difficult to spray powder on fruit trees in order to kill the pests that loved fruits as much as we did. Crop dusting by aerial spraying was not something the communist regime did. There was plenty manual labor around. The population needed employment in spite of the meager wages. Workers dusted or sprayed the chemicals themselves without masks or any protection for that matter.

I do not remember ever eating a fruit that did not have worms in it. Fruit flies deposited their eggs that grew into tiny, white worms that wiggled out of cherries, apples, pears, prunes, peaches, apricots as we took bites out of them. We could try to extricate the worms by cutting the fruit into sections without parasites in them, or could just eat it whole and unwashed, not worrying or thinking about the worms. They constituted, after all, extra protein, and we were starved for protein all the time. We were not vegetarians by choice. Meat was so hard to find except at Christmas time when country folks slaughtered pigs and the government supplied stores in town with extra meat in order to pacify the starving urban proletariat.

There were a few orchards slated for communist elite consumption or export and those were tended to carefully. The fruit was whole and untouched by parasitic fruit flies.

During Christmas holidays, small shipments of oranges and bananas came from Greece, Israel, and people fought over them in long lines at the state grocery store. Such rare delicacies were rationed to a few pieces per family. We were so excited to get the exotic fruits and free of worms!

There were no ten-pound bags of oranges similar to those we buy at Sam's Club and no neat rows of perfect oranges or bunches of bananas like those that we find in American grocery stores every day. We take the abundance for granted because we have never experienced shortages of anything. We trust that whatever we need, will always be there, someone will grow them and ship them to our markets. But will they?

Mom finished her inspection of the "imperfect" banana. She threw it out with a huff, convinced that it had worms. Mom is blessed to have plenty of other food or fruits to satisfy her hunger. By the grace of God and a stroke of good luck, she lives in the land of plenty. She does not have to worry about her next meal. She has the luxury of throwing away good food that she mislabels wormy, tainted, or rotten. After all, there is so much food in this country and so cheap. Will we always be so lucky and have this luxury forever?

I Dream of Southfork

The late Larry Hagman was credited with saving Romania from communism. In a video clip, the actor who portrayed the infamous and villainous J. R. Ewing tells the story of a Romanian who approached him on a visit to the formerly communist country with tears in his eyes, "Thank you, J.R., for saving Romania."[37]

Millions of people around the globe tuned in from 1977 to 1991 to watch the TV show *Dallas* and the celluloid life of the fictitious Ewings, the oil rich tycoons, the detestable J.R., his alcoholic and co-dependent wife Sue Ellen, his honest brother Bobby, and all his sordid affairs.

I am not sure why the tyrant Ceausescu allowed us to watch *Dallas.* Perhaps he thought or was advised that this soap opera represented everything that was bad about capitalism and we needed one more reason to hate capitalism. Instead, we loved it!

Every weekend we tuned in faithfully, escaping for one hour from our imprisoned lives, glued to black and white TVs. The streets were empty, whole blocks would get together to watch the soap opera on the one TV screen that was larger and newer, and we prayed that the local government did not turn our electricity off. It was common occurrence to have blackouts – we had shortages of everything else, all the time, due to poor centralized planning by uneducated communist bureaucrats.

The ranch at Southfork became larger than life; its palatial surroundings made our concrete block apartments seem so small, that one could easily fit into Sue Ellen's well-appointed closet. I was disappointed when a Texan friend told me that the Southfork ranch was rather small. We had imagined a massive mansion with beautiful bedrooms and a huge kitchen stuffed to the brim with food. Southfork became a metaphor for freedom, abundance, and success through the opulent lifestyles of the *Dallas* characters.

We thought all Americans were rich like the Ewings and money grew on trees. We longed for and saw freedom through the eyes of a badly scripted soap opera that kept our poor and miserable proletariat mesmerized.

There was a love-hate relationship with the character of J.R., the all-around bad guy without a conscience who tortured his wife with his blatant infidelity.

When J.R. was shot by Kristen, everybody asked me who did it since we were watching episodes distributed ahead of everyone else in the world. My relatives, whom I was visiting, were quite disappointed when I did not know at the time the answer to the question of the day. "Who shot J.R.?"

Larry Hagman told the Associated Press, "I think we were directly or indirectly responsible for the fall of [communism.]" "They would see the wealthy Ewings and say, 'Hey, we don't have all this stuff."

I don't think J.R. Ewing helped overthrow communism at all, directly or indirectly, but it gave us hope that someday we could make it to America, the land of the free and the home of the brave. Our dreams could come true, and success could be within reach through hard work if only the communist party, its brutal regime, and the dictator Ceausescu were gone.

It took a long time to topple communism, from its initial creep after the forced abdication of the king in 1948, until 1989 when the dictator and his wife were executed for treason and other crimes against humanity. There were many who emboldened the millions suffering under the Iron Curtain to break the chains of communism – among them the Polish Pope, John Paul II and President Ronald Reagan. When people could hunger and suffer no more, the barbed wire fences and concrete walls were demolished, and justice was served.

Sadly today, people who were born, raised, and grew old under the welfare-dependent, freedom-robbing communism, never learned how to cope on their own and to be self-reliant. Those Romanians are now the pro-communism voices, joined by neo-communist and pliable youth who are naïve enough to believe in a failed and miserable utopia. The lessons of history fall by deaf ears.

A Sliver of Soap

I took the thin layer of leftover soap and tried to stick it to a new bar I had unwrapped. I never stopped to think why I've always done this. I don't throw away a bottle of liquid soap or a dispenser of lotion either – I cut it open and use up the last ounce.

I am not a miser or Scrooge on purpose, I think it goes back to the years of living under the communist regime when we were deprived of all basic necessities, things that Americans always expect to be plentiful and available. I never forgot the powerful lesson of need and deprivation.

The domestically produced "Cheia" soap was made of animal fat with a particularly unpleasant odor. We used it to bathe, to do laundry by hand, and to wash our hair. Few could afford the nicely fragranced "Lux" soap bar available on the black market or in foreign currency stores set up for visitors.

In a country where the medical system was socialized and "free," in order to do their job right and supplement their meager salaries, doctors accepted bribes in soap, shampoo, deodorant, cosmetics, perfume, and other expensive and hard to find items. Bribes to doctors still exist today but in the form of cash. Grocery stores and specialty stores carry an abundance of toiletries and other goods that used to be in short supply twenty-five years ago.

Hotel maids brought home leftover soap, shampoo, or deodorant bottles that foreign guests discarded from toiletry bags when checking out.

The garments washed in "Cheia" soap and air-dried on clothes lines smelled like wet dogs. If that was not bad enough, by the time they dried, they turned grey from dust and other pollutants in the air. In winter time clothes were stiff on the line.

Despite what environmentalists tell us, less developed countries and communist regimes are the worst offenders when it comes to air quality and purposeful degradation of air, soil, and water. All you have to do is look at China's record of environmental pollution.

Lacking bleach, we used to boil white garments on the stove in a huge cooking pot with melted soap in it, stirring occasionally with a stick to prevent clothes from burning. When garments faded, mom added a blue powder to the washing pot to revive dark colors.

We saw the communist apparatchiks take their laundry to the cleaners. We envied the luxury and secretly wished we could do it too.

We scrubbed dishes with a harsh white powder. We boiled water on the stove to launder bedding items. Sheets were scrubbed by hand in the tub until my young hands were raw – no latex gloves.

The iron was literally a piece of cast iron heated repeatedly on the stove - Grandma's version had hot coals inside. I had to be extra careful not to burn the sheets or Dad's shirts – they were too expensive to replace.

Because shampoo was very pricey and hard to find (it came packaged in small plastic squares for individual use), we washed our hair with "Cheia" soap in the sink. It was difficult to rinse the soap out completely; traces of whitish powder remained in the hair shaft and on the comb. We did not know hair dryers existed until we watched "Dallas" on TV. In winter time I bent over the gas stove, drying my hair over the open flame – I am still amazed that my mane did not catch on fire – I did singe the ends sometimes and my eyebrows.

Americans can find such a wide and cheap variety of products; unappreciative of the abundance, always wanting more, they are unhappy and gripe about how poor they are. We would have loved to find just one brand of fragrant bath soap, shampoo, and toothpaste. What a luxury that would have been!

We did not fathom the existence of a washing machine much less of a dryer or of a dishwasher. Women today still hang laundry outside, nobody owns a drier. If they did, they could not afford the electricity, the rates are sky-high, and the power is insufficient to run appliances simultaneously. Many people own a front-loading washing machine but the clothes come out extremely wrinkled and have to be ironed. The fabric is rough to the touch, not soft. A fragranced liquid detergent replaced the unpleasant communist era "Cheia" soap.

Deodorant was also scarce and quite expensive. There was a very good reason why people smelled – hygiene and grooming were costly and a luxury. Many did not have running water in their homes or a bathtub; Turkish baths were available in bigger towns. Cosmetics and grooming products were astronomically priced for the proletariat - we were all equally poor and smelly.

Shaving was a luxury and few women owned razors – au naturel was the norm and nobody complained. Men looked disheveled because it was painful to shave with dull razor blades every day.

The ultimate in luxury and financial well-being was to afford a kinky perm in a beauty shop. Hair was burned in tight curls for months before it grew back healthy again. Women's heads looked like sheep.

We are so spoiled in this country; people spend astronomical amounts for hair products, soap, cosmetics, deodorant, hair driers, laundry products, and machines that make life so much easier. Laundry services are affordable enough that many Americans can take their clothes to be professionally dry cleaned. The deprived society I grew up in would be very surprised at how little appreciation Americans have for their plenty.

I finally understood what my Grandmother meant when she used to tell us, every time we turned our noses to food we did not care for that much, or refused something she offered, "Are you tired of Good?"

The Starving Goose

"*We trade freedom for a gilded cage.*" – Anonymous

My friend sent me a story that explains quite succinctly what happens to people who are so eager to become enslaved to more government and to communist utopia.

A famous communist leader, having been aided by western powers to amass a sizable portion of a continent, gave his underlings a valuable lesson in power and control. He asked them to convene at his palace. His lecture was going to be taught just once – his time was too valuable to waste. The apparatchiks were directed to bring a goose to the seminar.

Each acquired a bird, built a sizable cage to house it, and proceeded to feed it well. On a given day, all gathered in the grand ballroom of the palace, carrying various cages.

Arriving fifteen minutes late for good measure, the leader entered the grand ballroom followed by a very thin goose. With each step he took, the goose reached in his pocket, begging for grain. Magnanimously, and with studied aplomb, he fed it one single grain from time to time.

The underlings stood up and congratulated each other for being there, applauding the presence of the great one. The dear leader asked them to open the cages and to release the geese. As soon as the geese sensed that the cage had been unbolted and they were free to go, the birds took off, ignoring their masters.

The only bird left was the dear leader's starving goose. Ever so attentive, she looked up to him with a sad face, waiting for her master to dispense one single grain of food.

"Do you see what happened if you fed them too much? They forgot who you were and no longer recognized you as their master. My faithful goose, fed just a few grains a day, enough to keep her from starving to death, is the most loyal bird."

The abject lesson of near starvation and meager dependency was the dear leader's recipe to lead a nation of blind and helpless followers.

The Kindergarten Booties

"Freedom's just another word for nothin' left to lose,
And nothin' ain't worth nothin' but it's free." – Kris Kristofferson's song

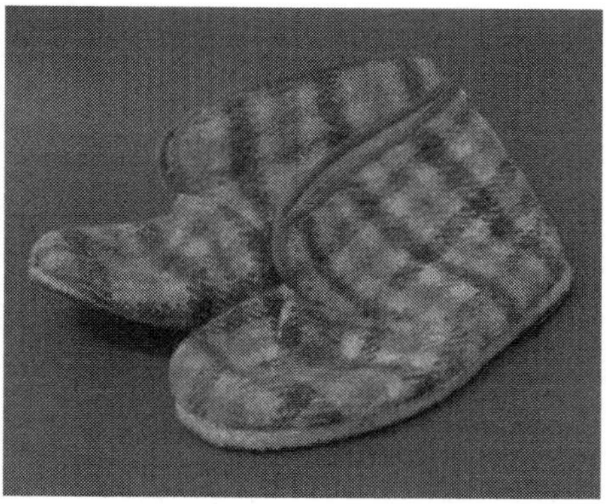

The photograph of a pair of kids' booties posted on a social website, "Copilaria anilor 80-90," triggered a flood of memories – it was the exact pair that I used to wear as a child. They were the only ones available for purchase, and required uniform for all children who attended pre-school and kindergarten.

I re-posted the photo thinking that a few of my Romanian friends would comment, but I was wrong. Instead, my much younger cousin from Romania remarked that she had a pair in pre-school in the 1980s. Who knew that commies would stick to the same sorry, cheap, and ugly pair of booties for decades?

One American lady, Gemey, who had traveled to Romania as a missionary in the 1990s, long after communism was temporarily dismantled, wrote, "Having grown up here in the U.S., it's difficult to imagine no electric, no water, no heat, little food, few clothes. I saw all that, well not the heat, no air conditioning in July was bad enough! But it's a beautiful country, reminds me of Virginia or Missouri where I live. Green and fertile and full of promise each day. And the people that I met were strong and resourceful and coped with all these situations with grace most of the time. But the moment things got a little better, people were clamoring for more, communist politicians promised more [just like the Bolsheviks] and they voted the commies back into office… sounds like the U.S. doesn't it?"

She continued, "Superstitions die hard. Even medical doctors believed that evil spirits blew into open windows and people would get sick if they walked barefoot." They also believed humans got sick if exposed to a slight breeze or draft. Consequently, kids had to wear these felt booties called "sosoni" or "botosei," crudely made and itchy, in pre-school and kindergarten.

Mom always yelled at me to put on house shoes and she always kept an assortment of slippers in her closet in the U.S. Her granddaughters were amused and loved to irritate her by going barefoot on any kind of surface.

It's hard to overcome any government dependency, even the communist variety. I have many older relatives who can barely make ends meet today because their pensions from the communist era are so small, yet they are nostalgic for communism. They want to live on the "take-care-of-me plantation," and "I will do as you say farm." Why try hard at all when everyone makes the same miserable salary?

The elderly today make an eager voting block that turns out every time to elect the communists back in power – the grey hair commie-voting brigade. They are like jail inmates who spend their entire lives in prison and, when freed, have no idea how to live on the outside, in the free world. They want back in prison where their needs were met poorly but were not expected to do much in return except be on their best behavior, be obedient to strict rules, and be willing to stay behind bars, the very bars that robbed inmates of their freedom in the first place.

I asked my cousin Maria why she voted for communists and she answered, they gave us a small pension, we did not have to work, the rent was low and subsidized, food was hard to find but was also subsidized, cheap alcohol was plentiful, we had rationing coupons, everyone was equally poor and miserable, we did not have to compete, we did not have to try very hard. We just understood that the commies in power were wealthy beyond belief but we accepted that as long as they threw us our daily crumbs and bones. We knew our place and they "protected" us.

What did they protect you from, I asked her. We had a miserable roof over our heads and medical care was free. But Maria, it was free, but you could not see doctors nor buy medicines because they were not available, shortages were constant, and you had to fight in lines for the last loaf of bread, toilet paper roll, or bottle of cooking oil, and you had to pay bribes in cash and goods to be seen on time by a better doctor. True, she said, but we had free aspirin and generic Tylenol. She looked down at her feet and remained silent. My arguments did not seem to penetrate her skewed view of reality. No matter what I said, if she had a choice, she would choose communism again and again, graciously resigned and happy with government dependency in exchange for empty promises and scratchy felt booties for her grandchildren.

Having seen the insidious welfare dependency under crony capitalism and under socialism/communism, I seriously doubt that I could change an elderly person's mentality of addiction to government handouts, even handouts not worth having.

My Christmas Tree

As long as I can remember, my Dad came home every December with a scraggly blue spruce, fragrant with the scent of winter, tiny icicles hanging from the branches. The frozen miniature crystal daggers would melt quickly on Mom's well-scrubbed parquet floor. I never knew nor asked where he had found it, or how he could afford it. His modest salary of $70 a month barely covered the rent, utilities, and food. Mom had to work as well to afford our clothes. Prices were subsidized by the government and salaries were very low for everybody regardless of education and skill. We had to make do with very little.

No matter how bare the branches of my Christmas tree were, it was magical to me. Two metal bars forged by hand helped Dad nail the tree to the floor at the foot of the couch where I slept in the living room that doubled as my bedroom. Our tiny apartment only had one bedroom where my parents slept.

Decorating it was a fun job every year since I made new decorations from colorful crepe paper. We had to be creative; we could not afford glass ornaments. We made paper cones covered with rolled crepe paper and filled with candy. I hung small apples with red string, tiny pretzels, home-made butter cookies, candied fruit, raisins, and an occasional orange wrapped in tissue paper with strange lettering, coming all the way from Israel. Each year we bought 12 small red and green candles which we attached to the tree with small metal clips. We were careful to clamp them at the tip of the branch to keep the tree from catching fire when the candles were lit. The tree would live for two weeks before the prickly needles fell all over the living room floor.

One year I spent Christmas with uncle Ion and his wife. A gifted mechanical engineer, Ion could fix and build anything. He promised that he would fashion lights for his Christmas tree. He worked painstakingly for weeks, soldering tiny copper wires into bundles that stretched along the branches of the tree like a magical cascade to which he soldered at least 200 tiny bulbs sold as bike lights. It was a labor of love! When the wires were finally attached to a relay, the bulbs lit up like a waterfall. Nobody had such a fantastically blazing tree in the whole country. I was amazed at his dedication and craftiness and never forgot his fairytale Christmas fir.

We did not have a tree skirt but we used one of Mom's hand-stitched table cloths. The whole apartment smelled like the fragrant mountains and, for a couple of weeks we forgot the misery that surrounded us. We lit up the 12 candles on Christmas Eve and on Christmas Day.

Every night for two weeks, I would admire my enchanted tree until I fell asleep, wondering what special treat I would find under my pillow on Christmas morning. It was never much, but it was such a cherished joy!

Saint Nicholas Day was celebrated on December 6th. We really didn't know much about the real St. Nicholas, Santa Claus's namesake. St. Nicholas was a popular saint in the Orthodox Church and presumed the bishop of Myra in Turkey in the 300s. There were many legends of St. Nicholas - the more famous story that he was the son of a wealthy family in Patara, Lycia. When his parents died, he gave away his fortune. One such random act of kindness involved throwing three bags of gold through the windows of three girls who were going to be forced into prostitution.

On Saint Nicholas Day, I would put my boots outside the door, hoping that they would be filled with candy in the morning and not coals. Grandpa had a wicked sense of humor – he would sometimes fill one boot with sticks and another with candy and a chocolate bar.

Grandpa never bought a blue spruce - we cut a fir tree from the woods. We were careful not to cut down a tree that had bird nests in it. We decorated it with garland made from shiny and multi-colored construction paper. We cut strips, glued them in an interlocking pattern and voila, we had our garland. For ornaments we used walnuts and shriveled apples from his cellar, tied with Grandma's red knitting wool.

The warm adobe style fireplace built from mud bricks mixed with straw cast a dancing glow on the tree decked with tokens of food, something our heathen Roman ancestors did during the celebration of Saturnalia. On December 17, the polytheistic Romans celebrated Saturnus, the god of seed and sowing, for an entire week. As Christians, we celebrated the birth of Christ and the religious traditions in our Orthodox faith, in spite of the communist regime forcing the transformation of Christmas into a secular holiday.

On Christmas Eve, after we ate Mom's traditional Christmas supper, roasted pork, baked chicken, sarmale (stuffed cabbage rolls with ground meat and rice), and mamaliga (corn mush with butter cooked in a cast iron pot), we went to the midnight service at the Orthodox Church not far from our house. Sometimes it was a sloshy trek and other times it was icy and slippery. If we got lucky, a heavy snow would turn our walk into a winter wonderland with dancing snowflakes shining in the weak street lights. We had to bundle up well – the church was not heated and we circled it three times during the procession with burning candles in our hands. I always wore my flannel pajamas under many layers of warm clothes. To this day, pajamas are my favorite garment – cozy and comfortable, keeping my body warm.

I decorate my Douglas fir with beautiful lights and shiny ornaments now. My heart fills with loving memories of Christmases past and of family members lost who made our Christian traditions so special even during the dark times of communism.

My Perfect Christmas Treats

On December 6, all children waited anxiously the arrival of Saint Nicholas, the old bearded man with ragged clothes. Everyone put their shoes outside the door in hope that they would be filled with candy and chocolate.

Many did not know the story of Saint Nicholas, the Bishop of Myra from Turkey. The story goes that he had become the symbol of anonymous gift giving when he donated three sacks of gold to an old man whose daughters could not marry because he was so poor, he could not afford dowries. St. Nicholas threw a bag of gold each night into the old man's house through an open window. When the story was told in colder climates, St. Nicholas dropped the gold through the chimney.

St. Nicholas came to represent secret gift giving. He was portrayed in meager clothes with three round discs, the three sacks of gold. In the town of Bari, Italy, where the Bishop was buried, pawnbrokers hung three gold disks in front of their shops in remembrance of St. Nicholas' gift of gold.

Eastern Orthodox churches celebrate services on the night before December 6 when St. Nicholas appears as a bishop, not in a red suit. Parishioners leave their shoes outside the door and, upon departure, find gold disks of chocolate wrapped in foil inside their shoes, in remembrance of the three gold dowries that St. Nicholas provided to the poor man.

My childhood friends in Romania left their galoshes outside the door. The one pair of leather boots each of us owned in winter was too precious to leave out in the elements. We wore galoshes over boots in order to protect them from rain and the dirty slosh when snow began to melt. We trusted that nobody was interested in taking our rubber galoshes.

Every morning on December 6, I would find an exquisite orange, a banana, a large chocolate bar filled with raisins, and a small bag of hard candy. I felt very special and was always curious why I could never catch St. Nicholas bringing the food.

The communist economy we lived under never delivered enough basic and decent food for everyone, much less luxuries such as fresh fruit in winter. A banana or an orange were exquisite gifts of food that we dreamed about all year long.

People waited in long lines for the lone salami in the window of a butcher shop. Unlike the privileged elite that shopped at their own stores, we had to contend with empty shelves and long lines. To pacify the masses at Christmas time, the communist party leaders would order extra food, fresh fruits, and the lines were shorter.

December 25 was a secular holiday with "Mos Craciun," Santa Claus, who was dressed in red with a fake cotton beard. We still believed, however, that he had the power to place a small gift by our pillow the night before. I would wake up to find a small rag doll with a porcelain head, a book, or a small puzzle.

Although the communist party did not allow people to go to church, we always went to my Grandmother's village for Midnight Mass on Christmas Eve, circling the church with lit candles three times for the Holy Trinity.

Groups went caroling from house to house at night and were received with gifts of food, hard pretzels, or a warm cup of plum brandy. No matter how hard the communists tried to suppress our traditions, faith survived.

Magically, a tree decorated with real candles, colorful handmade crepe paper baskets filled with candy, hanging apples, cookies, and a few ornaments appeared. The glass ornaments must have cost my Dad a fortune since they were hard to find. The Christmas tree did not have electric lights, but we would light up candles carefully for a short while on Christmas Eve. The scent of the blue spruce filled our small home and made me happy. I was walking on air, oblivious to my parents' financial sacrifice.

Nobody exchanged presents, the holiday was about our faith in God, children, togetherness with the extended family, visiting each other's homes, eating and drinking whatever we had. Villagers slaughtered pigs for Christmas and shared them with family members. The leftovers were preserved in a cellar or smoked to feed them throughout the year when meat was hard to find.

Eating chocolate was an acquired taste. Grandpa convinced me to try the gooey confection I melted on the heater to spread on my doll's face. I was playing house and feeding my doll chocolate. Grandpa never told me how many bars of chocolate I ruined this way. Once hooked, chocolate became a favorite treat for special occasions.

My Christmas banana was always green and I had to wait until it turned golden and sweet. I placed both fruits in the middle of the table so I can see them from every angle in the room. The orange was wrapped in white onionskin paper. I kept it for days admiring its perfect orange color and the fragrant smell emanating from its pores. It came from a faraway place, Israel, whose language I could not read.

I wondered what exotic place grew such perfect fruits and how long it took to travel to me. Will I ever journey to see the tree and pick this perfect orange myself? The wind was always howling outside and the snow was coming down very hard but I was dreaming of the tropical location that grew my perfect Christmas treats.

Leaving China to Find Freedom, Fresh Air, and the Good Life in Eastern Europe

Li Bing Zhi left his native China to become a goat herder in the village of Lacusteni in southern Romania. His animals produced milk and cheese for Chinese restaurants in the capital Bucharest. He traded his forceps of an OBGYN in China for a shepherd's staff. His wife, a mathematics professor, and his son were still in China.

He tried his hand at raising pigs first but the business went belly up because the pigs were not gaining weight fast enough in spite of the nutritious feed. In China, pigs gained 100 kilos in six months. He decided instead to grow Chinese vegetables, cabbage, and to raise 150 goats with his associate's father.

Constantin Dragan and Dan Mihalacea, reporters for Realitatea TV, interviewed Li Bing Zhi in February 2011. In broken Romanian and a jocular mien, Li Bing explained that he paid his workers well when they showed up for work. After they drank their pay at the end of the month, they returned to work sheepishly. Since they were so undependable, Li Bing bought a few dogs that he trained himself. Li Bing gave his goats Romanian names like Monica, Tantica, and Tapul.

Most villagers accepted their new neighbor with open arms and called him "our Chinese." A small group, however, were not impressed with him and resented the fact that his goats ate the grass that nobody used or needed anyway but that was not the point. He was intruding on no man's lands, grazing his goats in the woods and other pastures, and he did not belong in their village. Besides, he worked very hard and earned good money, a source of envy and discord.

Three years ago, Li Bing Zhi opened a business in Bucharest. When it failed, he moved with one of his associates to her native village of Lacusteni de Sus. What was his explanation for settling in such an unlikely place, far away from his native China and his family?

Li Bing traded the pollution and restrictions of communist China for fresh air, freedom, and a good life in the formerly communist country of Romania, more capitalist today than many countries in Western Europe. He said, he wanted to settle there permanently - "Where else could I go? Maybe the cemetery?" I was a doctor in China but I now raise goats in Romania."

The case of this Chinese doctor fascinated me because he fled from a totalitarian state to a formerly totalitarian state. I judged his move through the prism of my experience. I have moved from a totalitarian state to the United States, which was the beacon of freedom at the time in late seventies, the "shining city on the hill." Today, considering the accelerated change towards socialism/Marxism and welfare dependency in the United States, would I move again to my adopted country, or would I choose perhaps a newly emerging capitalist country like Romania?

Freedom, fresh air, a good life are very tenuous gifts from God in any society. In 1989, when communism fell, Li Bing would not have chosen Romania as his permanent residence because it was just as oppressive, polluted, and poor as his native China was.

Change for the wrong reason and blind faith in an omnipotent government can take away fragile freedoms and an abundant life. Will we be able to keep our exceptional country based on successful capitalism and Judeo-Christian values? Will Romania be able to keep its fragile newfound capitalist freedom, good life, and fresh air?

That remains to be seen since communist agitators and community organizers are on the rise, supported by European socialists and communists that never went away; they just hid in plain sight and re-emerged in larger and larger numbers who are quite well financed.

1989 A Bittersweet Year

I watched recently the video of a speech given by the dictator Nicolae Ceausescu to an adoring crowd of communist useful idiots a few days before the dictator was arrested in December 1989. Ceausescu, a megalomaniac who appointed himself the Father of the Country, was touting the slave wages he had ordered raised for his unlucky proletariat from 700 lei per month to 800 lei.

At the time, the pegged exchange rate was 12 lei to a dollar, making the proletariat's wage of $58 per month go up to $67. What could we buy with this money? Sixty-seven dollars per month bought us subsidized teacup-sized concrete block apartments, occasional heat, some electricity, daily-scheduled hot or cold water, subsidized weekly bus fares, one pair of shoes per year, one outfit, and enough food to keep us from starving to death. Most of us were underweight and malnourished, in dire need of vitamins which were impossible to find on the empty pharmacy shelves.

"To each according to his ability, to each according to his needs," said Karl Marx's popular slogan, "Jeder nach seinen Fähigkeiten, jedem nach seinen Bedürfnissen." Ceausescu and his wife and the communist party elites had been the deciders of our needs since March 22, 1965 until December 25, 1989.

The year 1989 was a painful, bittersweet period in my life and in the history of my people. It was a year filled with death, life, grief, anguish, freedom, physical pain, and the struggle for power.

My father passed away on May 12 in excruciating pain, denied drugs, IV nourishment, and any kind of medical treatment, an 80-pound shadow of his former self. My Dad was a sturdy and healthy 200 pound man full of life and joie de vivre.

An outspoken critic of the president, Dad was always detained at his place of employment for his views, his lack of membership in the communist party, and his not-so-secret desire to have another president replace Ceausescu in his lifetime.

Dad had just turned 61 when he was beaten one last time and languished three weeks before his death in a hospital ward, tended by his loving sister who kept him alive with teaspoons of water and broth. My Dad was one of thousands of victims, killed by communists in their quest for power and control. His honesty, his integrity, his freedom of speech, and his desire to be free sentenced him to an early demise.

Dad passed away one day before my doctoral graduation. He was so proud that his only child could accomplish something he had dreamed of – the opportunity to excel in a free country. I dedicated my degree to my Dad, to his unwavering support for my education. My mortarboard read "4 Dad" but it was little consolation for the visceral pain and inconsolable loss I felt.

President George Bush Sr. handed me my diploma, shook my hand, and later wrote a very touching letter about my father. It was a bittersweet accomplishment. While I knew my Dad was in Heaven, smiling upon my shoulders with every ray of sunshine, I was angry that an innocent, sweet man was taken from this Earth before his time by the evil forces of communism.

Daddy had died holding a crumpled photograph of me and his two granddaughters in our finest Easter dresses. It was the only possession he was allowed to keep.

Dad's nemesis did not live much longer. Ceausescu and his harpy wife Elena were sentenced to death and executed on Christmas 1989, ending their 24-year reign of terror. It was the first time during the communist regime that Christmas carolers and the midnight Christmas service were televised from the Patriarch's Cathedral. The Orthodox Christians could finally worship freely without fear of reprisals.

Caught in the town of Tirgoviste while trying to flee by helicopter, the husband and wife team who had terrorized an entire nation for 24 years, bringing its people to their knees and to utter desperation, were now facing a military tribunal tasked with judging and sentencing them.

Refusing to answer questions based on the Constitution that he wrote, the dictator Nicolae repeated that he would only answer to the Grand National Assembly, not to the assembled military court. After a speedy, improvised, and bizarre trial that lasted one hour, during which the couple refused to cooperate, did not answer most questions, or gave canned propaganda answers, they were sentenced to death in front of a firing squad and their wealth confiscated.

Their 24-year reign of terror ended when a peaceful rally for a persecuted pastor in the western town of Timisoara led to a national uprising. The Ceausescus were captured shortly after they fled their home. The fighting continued between those loyal to the dictator and the population. According to Corneliu Lemnei, eyewitnesses saw the dictator's personal army appear early in the night from underground tunnels, shooting unarmed people randomly, a painful reminder that the unarmed population with no right to bear arms were target practice for the armed-to-the-teeth presidential private army.

The mercenaries Ceausescu had hired, shot and killed, by some estimates, thousands of innocent Romanians who had gathered to protest peacefully the oppressive communist regime at the palace in Bucharest. The secret police executed many innocents in surprise raids, including doctors, nurses, and patients in hospitals.[38]

The Romanian Army finally had had enough and joined civilians to fight against the communist tyranny.

"Why did you starve the people to death?" "I will not answer that question," the deposed President said.

How can you make two narcissists, blinded by communist ideology, by absolute power and control, who made themselves wealthy beyond anybody's imagination at the expense of the misery of the proletariat they so pretended to care about, understand the crimes they've committed against the Romanian people? As the prosecution said, it was "genocide through famine, lack of heat, lack of light, but the worst crime of all, the crime of imprisoning the Romanian spirit."

I wished my Dad had lived to witness the joy the Romanian people experienced when the dictator was finally executed on Christmas Day 1989. Watching a soldier tie the wrists of the humiliated couple with plain rope and their outrage and claim that he cannot do that to "the Mother and Father of the Country" was vindication for the many times my Dad had suffered indignities, beatings, arrests, and eventual death for his political views.

One individual commented that the Romanian people should have been allowed to be part of the trial and of the final punishment in the streets. But everyone was eager to get rid of the scourge of communism and of those who forced such dehumanizing ideology on an entire nation.

The fight for power ensued; the communists changed their stripes, became wealthier, joined the European Union, while their overt leaders went underground. Communists resurfaced with a vengeance in recent years, aided by European Fabian socialists and communists flush with money.

Uncle Ion and Grandma's Orchard

In the fall of 2012 I was on a mission to see my Dad's last three surviving siblings, two sisters and a brother. First on the list was Uncle Ion, my Dad's youngest brother. Had my Dad lived to a ripe old age, he would have probably looked very much like his sibling. When they were kids, Dad helped raise Ion and was his role model, especially after Grandma Elisabeta became a widow with eight kids at such a young age.

Ion turned 78 in 2013 and lived in Grandma Elisabeta's house in Popesti, not far from the bustling city of Ploiesti, the center of the oil industry during the communist regime.

I drove the rented VW-Jetta through the sloping hills, dangerously close at times to the narrow ledge that separated the road from the deep ravines. The asphalt made it a quick and smooth journey unlike the long and bumpy ride of my childhood in the rickety communist bus that ran only twice a day, carrying a few workers back and forth to the village from their factory jobs and the occasional visitor to the city who needed medical attention. The Diesel engine fumes choked us through the open windows or the cracks through the doors. I could see the ground running along the route through the small rust holes on the floor board. The commies did not care that we rode like rodents in a rusty tin can. They had fancy and shiny Russian made Volgas with state paid chauffeurs.

We were thrown all over the bus every time it hit a pot hole and there were quite a few. Deep ruts cut during a heavy downpour by big rigs dried into uncomfortable and hard to navigate jarring tracks. When the road was muddy, the deep ruts made by previous vehicles stalled the bus. The men got out and pushed until the wheels stopped spinning and the bus got traction again. Nobody cared that they were caked in mud; they were already dirty from their factory jobs. I always felt bad for them. At least in the drab grey apartments in the city we had a tub and a sewer system. Even if the water was not running or was cold, we could carry buckets from other streets or we could heat it on the stove as long as the natural gas had not been turned off. We felt like royalty because we could bathe once a week. The poor villagers had to carry water from wells far away. It was thus precious, used for cooking and drinking. People went to bed dirty and got up the next day and dressed in the same clothes. It was hard work doing laundry by hand at the river.

I drove by the stream where we bathed in summertime and washed our clothes. Nothing seemed to have changed that much. The landscape is easily recognizable – I can almost see myself running through the tall weeds followed by my cousins, racing to be the first one in the cold water. A couple more hills and I arrived in the center where the bus stop used to be. It's still there, clearly marked by a shiny painted sign. Across the road, the small state-run store that sold mostly alcohol, sugar, flour, corn meal, and a type of dried up pretzels called "covrigi" is gone, replaced by a new building with a modern façade, large windows, and a neon sign. It was so frivolous and verboten to have large windows during the dark and energy-starved era of Ceausescu's tyrannical communism. I stopped and peered inside. Neon lights, ads on a flat screen TV, a large freezer and a refrigerator held any imaginable item a convenience store would have and some. To my surprise, cousin Gigi owned the store. Still a relatively young man, his entrepreneurship paid off in the free market system. Remnants of the old communist system remained in the bribery and the overt political corruption. Gigi sold t-shirts, rented DVDs, meats, fish, cheese, dairy, candy, oil, wine, pastries, canned goods, and other foods that villagers could only dream of once. Abundance was here within their grasp. The second floor held a cozy restaurant/bar that served local dishes and beer.

Homes looked larger, more substantial, better maintained, with a car parked up front and intricate wrought-iron fencing; yet most still did not have running water. What was the point in having a bathroom with a tub if there was no sewer system or a septic tank?

Some houses looked shuttered, the owners gone somewhere in the European Union working hard for a year to bring home euros, save them, buy a car, pay for a wedding, buy a few pigs, cows, goats, or add another floor to the villa.

The steep hill in front of me had been blacktopped as well – no more trudging through mud. A few goats were grazing in the ditch, having escaped their enclosures. I decided to walk uphill to uncle Ion's house. It was the same I had remembered. The weathered wood fence hid the tall fruit trees and the grape vines. The rusty metal gate looked like it had not been painted in years. A clothes line ran parallel with the gravel walkway and sported a few plastic grocery bags hanging out to dry. Nothing is discarded; everything is still reused, rewashed, repaired, and refurbished, just like under communism when nobody could afford to be wasteful.

The house was the same stucco, half painted white and the other half a bright teal. Huge cracks along the side made it look like it was leaning. The wooden door was also painted teal. The small porch banister was peeling teal paint. I spent many days on this porch watching nature unfold in front of me, listening to the buzzing of bees, and counting bright stars at night. It was on this porch that my Dad's and Grandma Elisabeta's coffins were placed before the last journey to their resting place in the village cemetery. I peeked through the window of the room where Grandma used to sleep. The furniture was nicer and was very familiar; it was the furniture that belonged to my parents. Perhaps Dad had willed everything to uncle Ion. The packed dirt floor I knew, expertly swept by Grandma Elisabeta every day, had been replaced by poured concrete, covered by a handmade wool rug. A crucifix with prayer beads was the only ornament on the wall. It was Grandma's favorite; the beads were made of polished garnet and blessed by the Mitropolit, the leader of the Orthodox church.

I checked the other room, nobody was inside, it looked like a kitchen/storage room full of jars, bottles, dishes, and various small tools. I turned around, ready to leave, when I heard the creak of the metal gate. A very thin old man with hollow cheeks walked towards me. It was uncle Ion. I recognized his bright blue eyes. Half of the children inherited Grandma's beautiful blue eyes and the other half had green eyes like my Dad. Uncle Ion was wearing tattered clothes and his pants were held up by a string. I flinched in dismay. It was Sunday and he did not look like he worked in the garden. I knew he had a good pension but he never spent it on himself – he supported his unemployed daughter and her two children. Unemployment hit hard the former communist countries like Romania who joined the European Union in 2007. Uncle Ion was too old to take advantage of the new economic opportunities; he was satisfied with his pension.

His daughter quickly became the typical product of the European entitled welfare nanny state. I felt sorry for uncle Ion - I wanted to go buy him some clothes but he proudly declined. He was happy and content in his self-imposed poverty like a penitent monk.

Happy to see me, almost incredulous that I was there after 25 years, he kept digging in his pocket looking for his glasses that were obviously lost. We sat on the steps for a few hours, talking and remembering all relatives, dead and alive. My husband was a bit overwhelmed, not because he felt left out when he could not understand our conversation (he got the jest of it) but because this level of poverty, need, and misery was alien to him. He could not understand why people have not made more progress in 25 years since the "fall" of communism, why the former commies still live so well and are in charge, while ordinary people like uncle Ion were still so very poor? My hubby did not understand that uncle Ion chose to live this way because he wanted to support his daughter who did not work, and his grandchildren.

I tried to convince uncle Ion to let me erect a marble monument on my Dad's tomb. Ion's wife Angela is buried on the same plot and I offered to carve her name and photograph on a double monument. Ion refused my offer. As the only surviving senior male of the Apostolescu clan, he was de facto owner of the cemetery plot and I could not convince him unless I bribed him generously. Bribery still greased the wheels for everything in a country where most citizens learned to survive for forty years under communism through bribery, "borrowing" from work, and barter – old habits die hard. I would have offered whatever monetary compensation he was asking for but I knew the money was not going to benefit him in any way. I resented the lack of industriousness in young people and the entitled attitude that they were too good or too educated to work on menial or ordinary jobs.

Uncle Ion started to cry when we stood up to leave, it was almost dark. Last time I saw him he was young, vibrant, and defiant. He would have moved mountains to protect and care for his family.

He had aged and mellowed a lot but was the same lively character with twinkly blue eyes. He picked a few plums and peaches from Grandma's orchard and stuffed them in a well-worn paper bag, handing it to me. It was Grandma's routine when I went for a visit. She always sent me back to the city with a bag full of fruits and vegetables. The purple plums were plump, juicy, sweet, and fragrant just as I remembered them in my dreams, scaling fences and climbing trees in the orchard and picking my own fruits.

I turned around and gazed at the silhouette holding on to the garden gate. I wanted to sear this moment into my memory. I was not sure if I would see uncle Ion again. In the twilight, his smile looked eerily similar to my Dad's when I last saw him. He waved good-bye as the car sped off and my childhood orchard disappeared from sight.

On the drive back to the city, I gave the wheel to my husband. My eyes were filled with tears of regret and longing for a time and life that no longer existed, for family members who were now just a loving memory. I was distracted by the running landscape, the sheep and goats crossing the road, the orange sunset, the pungent smell of crushed grapes, and the cherished images of people and places playing through my mind's eye.

A Cow, Wisdom, and Economics

I have always learned from the wisdom of my senior generations. As a child, I sat spellbound in the twilight around the elders of the village, listening to their stories. The lessons learned were priceless and fascinating for someone who "had not seen the world yet." The moral of those long ago and faraway sagas have served me well through life.

I was delighted when, Ionel Iloae, a Romanian journalist, told a humorous story, albeit dark humor, of an entire village in Dragata, Moldova, who ate a "mad" cow. He was not talking about mad cow disease or Kreutzfeldt-Jakob syndrome, but a cow that had been bitten by a rabid animal, presumably a fox.

The drama started with a family's cow breaking a window and exhibiting the strange behavior of kicking the walls of the barn. Frightened, the Chiriacs called in the veterinarian, Robert Ciubotaru. After the cow was immobilized, the vet took blood samples and warned the family to stay away, as he was suspecting that the cow was infected with rabies.

The rabies virus is a neurotropic virus that causes fatal disease in humans and animals, the transmission occurring through saliva, hence the speculation that the cow had been bitten by an already infected animal.

A cow is a very precious and lucrative commodity on a Romanian farm. Why let such an opportunity go to waste? The wife decided to slaughter the animal before it expired, cook part of it for her family, and sell the rest to the village for 10 lei a kilogram. Word spread like wildfire and the villagers came in droves to buy fresh meat sold so much cheaper than the going price. Some, who left empty-handed and disappointed when the meat ran out, did not realize how lucky they were.

By sun down, Elena Chiriac sold all the beef, about 200 kilos. The village police officer bought some too but the mayor left disappointed. People all over the village had a feast and enjoyed their fresh beef. Elena cooked the liver immediately - it was her favorite dish.

The next morning, the results of the blood test came in. The cow was rabid and everybody had to turn in the meat bought the previous day. A large hole was dug up, the leftover meat was thrown in with a good dose of diesel and a fire was lit up until every piece of the poor animal was burned.

I never liked or ate beef personally – cows were always pets for me. My Grandparents kept them for dairy purposes. We milked them and made butter and cheese. Cows had a good and long life on our farm; they always died of old age, not disease. Only then were they sent to the city slaughterhouse.

Twenty-five people admitted that they had consumed the infected meat, the rest of the villagers were too ashamed. Only the fear of a painful death by rabies convinced the rest to submit to immediate vaccination. The mayor and the prefect had to obtain special dispensation for immediate delivery of all the necessary vaccines or the entire village would die.

The remorseful Elena, who knew better, but was more interested in the economics of her cow than the safety of her neighbors, hid in shame. A retired teacher and a village elder, everybody trusted her.

The incubation period of a rabies infection is 20 to 90 days. If the vaccine is administered immediately, there are no dangers. The virus enters through saliva and micro-lesions in the skin. After 30 days from infection, the disease becomes fatal. There are some cases in Africa of a rabies strain in the Yellow Mongoose where the animal can live asymptomatic for years.

The Director of DSV in charge of the food supply and animal safety did not assign blame to anyone. "The woman is not responsible that her cow got sick. We will assess the situation and pay the owner for the cow. We found the rabies in time, people are being vaccinated, and the risks are minor."

As Ionel Iloae so aptly describes it, in Moldova everything is handled with kindness – even a potential "small accidental genocide." The whole story would make a perfect comedy of errors plot.

Most people, who lined up at the village dispensary in a state of agitation to be vaccinated, admitted, "It was an issue of national interest." Some villagers have refused the vaccine. From a family of eight who ate the tainted beef, only one person admitted to have eaten the meat, and time was running out to vaccinate everyone.

The moral of the story is that greed driven by irresponsible economic "desperation" can be fatal.

Rationed Food and Purposeful Starvation

A bread line
Photo courtesy of the web

I remember our daily food always coming from long, long lines everywhere, at the end of which was a loaf of bread, a liter of milk, a stick of butter, a bottle of murky cooking oil, or a kilo of bones with traces of meat and fat on them.

The interminable lines looked like this bread line pictured here. We never knew what was sold at the end of the line we happened to come upon, but we knew we needed whatever people lined up to buy, so we joined the line.

If we wanted to eat, we learned at a very young age that we had to stand in long lines every day, often in bitter cold at 4 a.m. in hopes that the store would not run out of bread or milk by the time we made it to the front counter.

People carried cash and a shopping bag just in case they discovered hard to find items like toilet paper, aspirin, cotton balls, soap, potatoes, oranges, apples, flour, sugar, or cooking oil. From time to time, the shortage was so bad, we were issued rationing coupons. Once you ran out of rationing coupons for the month, you could not buy anything unless you were lucky enough to have extra cash to shop from the burgeoning black market of hoarders with communist party connections.

The ruling elite, of course, was fat and happy, shopping at their own grocery stores, usually located underground the local Communist Party headquarters.

It wasn't that the country did not produce enough food in spite of its disastrous centralized communist party planning. The mad dictator Ceausescu was determined to industrialize the country at the expense of people's food. He exported so much to the West in exchange for technology and hard currency that the Romanians had to make do with the leftover goods not fit for export.

The agricultural five year plan was developed by communist bureaucrats who were community organizers with very little experience at producing anything and very little formal education. They were schooled in the fine art of radical street agitation.

Around Christmas time and Easter, there was more food sent to stores, the lines were shorter for a few days and the stores better stocked. But that did not last very long. People would wipe out the supply in no time and the store shelves would be empty again, with one very expensive salami hanging behind the counter or in the window, buzzed by flies.

But that was nothing compared to the Soviet plan to starve the Romanian population of Bessarabia in 1946-1947 in order to achieve collectivization. According to the 1897 census, almost 48% of the population was Moldovan and thus spoke Romanian. Bessarabia and Northern Bucovina were Romanian-held prior to the military occupation by the Soviet Red Army during June 28-July 4, 1940. To avoid a military conflict, Romania withdrew from the area following a Soviet ultimatum delivered on June 26. The Romanian province was recaptured by Ion Antonescu from 1941-1944 and then reoccupied by the Soviets in 1944. The regions were subsequently incorporated into the USSR.

I recently came across an eye-witness 25 minute documentary by Bogdan Parlea, "Marturii Despre Suferintele Romanilor din Basarabia" ("Witness to the Suffering of the Romanians in Bessarabia"), produced by the **Fundatia Sfintii Inchisorilor** and **Fundatia Parintele Arsenie Boca**. Hundreds of thousands of Moldovans died at the hands of their Soviet Socialist tormentors who confiscated their crops by force and shipped the food to USSR. Wheat and corn was left to rot and mold in uncovered wagons at train stations; it was done to leave farmers as poor and desperate as possible in order to better manipulate and control them.[39]

According to Alexandru Moraru, the gazette "Moldova Socialista" ("Socialist Moldova") reported on January 28, 1947 that the food industry in the region had exceeded butter production by 33.2 percent, meat production by 32.5 percent, and canned food by 101.9 percent. This was the food confiscated from the starving Moldovans who were too weak to bury their own dead.[40]

It was a Soviet state secret - nobody was allowed to write or speak about the horrors that took place in Chisinau, Orhei, Balti, Cahul, and other villages, how collectivization agents took the last drop of food and grain from the farmer's barns, and how the children of Moldova were kidnapped, brought into homes, murdered, cooked, and eaten.

Survivors were interviewed as eye witnesses to the communist power which forced peasants to pay confiscatory taxes as well as huge quantities of their crops to the Soviet state, leaving them with little to eat. The small crop yields resulting from a very dry growing season coupled with the forced confiscation in the name of collectivization caused mass famine. Ten percent of the 1.5 million population died of starvation and a large percentage that survived were severely malnourished, looking like Holocaust victims.

Anatolie Iov Spinei described how the crop yield in 1946-1947 was only 500-600 kg per hectare due to the draught that year and the forced quota to the Soviet state was also 500-600 kg.

Eugenia Ciuntu described how her family dug a large barrel in the ground and hid grain inside but the Soviet community organizers came with sticks and tapped the ground, finding the barrel in the soft dirt. They were tapping everywhere, even hay stacks, in an attempt to find every last drop of grain.

Petre Buburuz, Orthodox Priest, explained that the end game was to starve and kill as many peasants as possible, take their land, and establish the Soviet collectives, the "colhoz." He described how people kidnapped other people and sold them for meat.

Margareta Spanu Cemartan talked about the "communist ideology to scare people, to bring them to desperation," to make them acquiesce to become part of the collectivization when faced with the prospect of dying. Farmers turned in their pre-determined quota of grain to the waiting trains, received a receipt, and then the communist agents came back for a second round of quotas, forcing them to sweep the last kernels of wheat and corn from their barns and give up their last chicken, cow, or pig. They were left with 8 children and nothing to feed them.

What did they eat? How did they survive? Parents fed their children first and chose to die the swelling and painful death of starvation. Nadejda Botea told how some men ground tree bark to feed their families. Valentina Sturza said that those found hiding food, were sent to Siberia 10-15 years in labor camps. Some survived by boiling non-poisonous weeds.

Ion Moraru said that every family had to turn in a certain quantity of everything that was produced on a farm, eggs, meat, grain, milk, cheese, wool, but not all peasants had all of these, so they had to pay extra taxes to make up for the shortage of food quota. Many were taken to the police precinct and beaten.

Those in charge of the collective farms were afraid to tell Stalin and his henchmen that the crop had been poor because of the draught. Consequently, the quotas were not adjusted to reflect the low crop yield.

People were so desperate to eat, they sold everything of value, icons, gold items, carpets, windows, doors, silverware, candlesticks, rosaries, including the clothes off their backs. According to Anatolie Iov Spinei, "Bread had become the currency. A carpet was worth a loaf of bread."

Teodosia Cosmin talked about eating weeds. Her mom sold every piece of clothing in her daughters' dowry trunks in order to survive.

Anastasia Ursachi talked about farmers keeping cows and goats in the house with them otherwise they were stolen and eaten. "Women carried babies to term, killed them, and fed them to the other children," she said.

They ate all dogs and cats. Nadejda Botea described how a woman's husband passed away; she put the body in the attic and fed him daily to her children. The weak were robbed of their food and possessions, so deep was the desperation.

Those who did not engage in cannibalism, were so weak, they were unable to bury their dead. They dragged them into mass graves and abandoned them. Some died when the new crop came in and families ate too much.

After watching this shocking eyewitness documentary with film footage of that time period, I will never again look at food in the same way. The inhumanity exhibited towards their fellow men by heartless and desperate human beings who were trying to survive at all costs, including cannibalistic murder, is glaring and devastating evidence why tyrants and their communist lapdogs should never be allowed to take power again.

Sweet Lucy

Sweet Lucy moves painstakingly slow and carefully, her arthritis twisting her back in pain, forcing her to slow down. The sunshine turns her hair into a fiery mane, warming and soothing her painful arthritic joints. She sits down in her favorite chair on the patio, taking in the gentle breeze with a sigh of elation and a smile when she notices the ducks floating on the nearby pond.

The first 48 years of her life were very hard and deprived under communism. When she arrived here in 1980, she was so thin and malnourished - she looked like a skeleton, with sunken eyes and pallid skin. She never returned to Romania except for one brief visit. Her life was so much easier here and my beautiful daughters became our lives and her universe.

She looked back many times on her decision, analyzing everything; sometimes she had regrets, missing her siblings, but most of the time was happy to be free. She used to jump every time there was a knock on the door. She thought it was the police looking for her although she had done nothing wrong. She was re-living the totalitarian state and the dreadful treatment of its citizens under the brutal regime of Ceausescu.

She has fallen down a lot lately. She has not broken anything but has gotten some nasty bruises that are slow to heal. She still goes up and down stairs, making sure she does not miss a step. Sometimes she passes out on the patio from the heat, self-induced dehydration, or plain dizziness from old age. She is never thirsty or hungry. We remind her to drink water and force her to eat with us.

We nicknamed her Lucy a few years ago when she dyed her hair flaming red and the nickname stuck. Her real name is Mimi but her grandchildren call her Maia, like the Roman goddess of dew.

She used to move mountains with her energy, tirelessly taking care of everyone's needs but her own. She gets frustrated because she is so slow now and her hands are weak and unsteady.

Lucy dreams often that her legs will work again like they used to; she would visit her great grandson who lives so far away; if he lived nearby, she could take care of him, she says, instead of sending him to a nursery during the day. I am not sure, she would be up for the challenge but the desire is still there.

Her eyes are as sharp as ever. She complains that her cataract surgery 10 years ago was a total failure – the doctor had no idea what he was doing. Yet she can thread a needle in no time and make sewing repairs. I cannot even see to thread a needle with glasses on and am several decades younger.

Lucy stopped doing her masterful crocheting a decade ago. I don't know why she stopped – her macramé doilies were a work of art. Maybe she lost interest because nobody seemed to appreciate what she created. There was a store in Starkville that loved her work - she sold quite a few pieces over the years. It is sad that I've never learned how to do it when she tried to teach me. I saw one of Lucy's macramé doilies on my daughter's table when we visited. It surprised me and made me happy – one young person appreciates hand-made beauty.

Most Americans no longer understand or appreciate the painstaking art of counted-cross stitching, needle pointing, knitting, or crocheting. Everything is done by machines, uniform and without the creative flair of two gifted hands.

My cousin Mariana still makes paintings with her tiny cross-stitch needle and canvas. You cannot tell, it is not a painting, until you get up close to the picture. I bought several of her pieces last year and she had them framed. It was difficult bringing them back across two continents but it was worth it. The custom officers asked me what they were. It is masterful beauty sewn by hand, I said, a lost art in the U.S. They gave me strange looks and waved me on through.

Mom tells me often that it is going to rain during the night. She knows for sure because the moon has lost all its water, it is a crescent moon. We laugh at her astronomical assessment, but then a steady rain starts falling after midnight. Maybe it is coincidence but it happens too many times.

Lucy refuses to go to the doctor to have any more blood drawn. She read somewhere that she may be left without blood if he draws too many vials of her precious blood. What if her body can no longer produce it? She heard on her two favorite Romanian TV channels that it may be true.

It breaks my heart to see her so unsteady and her gait so shaky; she gets frustrated with herself and refuses help sometimes. She is beginning to mix our names up but she can still remember beautiful poetry from her childhood. She lives trapped between two worlds, the old world she left behind 35 years ago and the current reality. Watching constant TV from the old world, she often confuses events happening there with events happening here.

She has not been able to learn English; she just knew enough to get in trouble. The most memorable incident was the wedding of a close friend. Mom commented to a guest she had seen before, a rotund lady, "You look good, you so fat!" Mortified, I had to explain to the lady that in our culture, being fat was a compliment. Communists kept us so starved, food was rationed and very expensive, so if you were fat, that meant that you were doing well economically, you could afford food on the black market. She did not buy the story and avoided us like the plague. We stopped making excuses for Lucy; we just file every new incident under "Lucy's hilarious pearls of wisdom."

We sent Mom to college classes, our English professor neighbor offered to teach her, to no avail. She would return from class frustrated, complaining of real or imagined headaches, and vowing to go back to Romania. She depended 100 percent on us to translate everything. We thought the birth of her granddaughters would force her to learn English. Instead, she taught her granddaughters Romanian as soon as they started to speak a few English words. They knew at an early age that Maia does not speak English, and what language everyone spoke. On daily walks, the oldest granddaughter served as the official translator. As a three year old, she would stomp her foot when anybody addressed mom in English – "Maia speak no English!" Embarrassed at her plight, the teenaged girls asked Lucy not to speak Romanian too loudly in public. As they grew older, they were happy and proud that they knew another language.

Lucy took her favorite granddaughter on walks in the nearby cemetery – it was quiet, green, and peaceful. Eileen would ask her with childish innocence and naiveté, "Grandma when are you going to die so I can come visit you?"

Lucy can no longer travel by plane to see her country, her brother and sister. She refuses to use a wheelchair and it would be futile to try to catch a flight while walking so painstakingly slow, she would never make it on time or people would knock her over. Besides, she has become scared of leaving home for distances further than the mall or her favorite neighborhood restaurant. She refuses to ride several hours to see her great-grandchild – perhaps when she feels better, she says, but that day never comes.

She talks to flowers and to our 13 year old Snowshoe Siamese cat Bogart as if they understand Romanian. Strangely though, Bogart still obeys her commands.

She still has the green thumb to bring flowers back from the brink of death. I watched her pick discarded dried roots intended for trash from the street; somehow she made a beautiful green plant grow back. She has nursed so many gardens and so many of us through the years! It frustrates her that she can no longer care for herself much less for us.

We know when she breaks something when we step on shards of glass or we look for the 20 year old crockpot with glass cover and find a strange metal lid on it. When we leave for a few hours, we know, when we return, she has already rearranged something in the house that did not suit her tastes.

I watch her struggle to wash her cup and teaspoon which she insists on doing and it makes me sad. She talks about past events with clarity as if they happened yesterday. She still talks to her younger brother and it makes her happy as if he is right there with her.

Lucy's world is so much smaller now, the house, the deck, and the patio. Tiny things in life, that we are too busy and too tired to notice, make her happy – the hummingbird in flight collecting nectar from her begonias, the deer that wonder into our back yard in the afternoon and eat the flowering tomatoes, the occasional fox that chases Bogart to our back door, the resident beaver in the nearby pond collecting twigs, the pair of Canadian geese that fly in and graze at the ridge of our yard, and the perfumed blooms of her favorite rose bush.

Mom is still full of life on the inside but her body is failing her and so is the scant and careless medical care she receives by various doctors we've visited – she is too old, they say.

On a beautiful fall day, September 17, 2014, Mom fell again and this time, after a lengthy hospital stay, she went into a nursing home. Mostly dependent on a wheelchair, Lucy is cared for by a staff who loves her. Her mind comes and goes, but she is the same optimist we love.

I see the vibrant, young Lucy who raised and loved so many of us, never asking for anything in return. She survived 48 years of communism, and lived well for 35 years in my house. Now she is at the mercy of a socialist medical care and I worry about her.

But I thank God that I still have my devoted Mom even though on some days she is confused, angry at the world, and scared.

"The Lives of Others"

"Das Leben des Anderen" is a 2006 German drama that describes in painful detail what life was like in the communist East Berlin of 1984, almost six years before the fall of the Berlin Wall, how ordinary and not so ordinary citizens were spied upon by their government, using agents of the infamous **Stasi**, the German Democratic Republic's secret police.[41]

The movie is not important because it showed how a famous actress was spied upon, her life, trials, and tribulations and the secondary minions who answered to the Kommunistische Partei (Communist Party). It is important because it shows the drab and meager daily life of fear, uncertainty, and horror that people in general endured under communist regimes.

Like the actress in the movie, homes were bugged; all telephone conversations were recorded and listened to. All incoming and outgoing mail was opened, read, and copied by small bureaucrats whose job was to report anything out of the ordinary and catalog their daily blogs.

The secret police did not have sophisticated wireless technology to spy on citizens like we have today. They also did not seek nor need warrants to record everything people did or said in their homes, cars, on the phone, social media sites, or by email. They had the oppressing power of government on their side and technology was not so advanced.

Passports were seldom issued for travel, however, when they were, travelers were highly scrutinized, their families held hostage, their meager possessions, and their bank accounts. There was no TSA or DHS with its modern technology but Stasi was equally successful. Instead, people were frisked and their bags searched when exiting large department stores. When everybody was so equally miserable, poor, and hungry, theft was a huge problem.

People under communism were asked to divulge to the Financial Police (a sort of IRS on steroids) what they owned, how much money they had hidden in the house, how they purchased certain goods, and why they ate sometimes better food than what was available on the market. Community organizers, not unlike ACORN, patrolled the streets, and, in exchange for better rations of food or a small monthly stipend, one individual was assigned per bloc of apartments to record the comings and goings into each apartment.

GPS tracking today in our smart phones, cars, boats, appliances, cable TV, cameras, social sites, credit card purchases, wireless smart meters, online purchases, flights, and reward/special customer grocery store shopping enable faceless individuals to track us and our lives daily.

If you have Verizon phone and cable service, a judge just ordered them to turn over all their data daily to the federal government to be stored without a warrant or a reason. Perhaps you think you are safe from this intrusion. The NSA data storage center in Bluffdale, Utah can handle a lot of storage, estimated to be 5 zettabytes of information.

Satellites can take pictures with extreme accuracy. Drones can spy in your bedroom as you sleep. Smart meters relay information to the mother ship about your gas, electricity, water consumption, your appliances, whether you are home, if you are using medical devices, and sports equipment. Appliances can talk to the grocery store and place food orders for you. Utilities companies can turn off your electricity, water, A/C, and gas whether you want it turned off or not.

IRS, who abused its authority many times, will now be in charge of your most sensitive medical information, with the power to deny medical care once the 15-member death panel is fully staffed and to control your most sensitive medical information.

Your boss monitors your email usage and content and blocks your access to certain sites. Businesses owned by people with liberal leanings firewall sites that contradict their views. YouTube takes down videos that offend liberals, thus stifling freedom of speech. Academia censors conservative professors by denying them tenure. Facebook censors conservative users constantly, no matter how polite their posts are. My own website has been censored on Facebook as spam.[42] Big publishers often turn down good conservative writers. The main stream media promotes political correctness and liberal views, preventing any polite opposition from exercising their freedom of speech.

If you consider how much territory political correctness occupies in the center of our lives and how much government bureaucratic control dictates what you do on a daily basis, do you still think you are free? Your brothers and sisters are watching you - they are empowered by non-elected government bureaucrats to spy on the "lives of others."

Fleeing Communism Only to Find It in America

As a legal immigrant, I came to America because it was "the shiny city on the hill" where everything was possible if you were willing to work hard because everyone had the freedom and equal opportunity to succeed.

I came to America because I wanted to pursue higher education, something that was very limited under communism as the children of the communist party elite had first choice at any college no matter how bad their grades were. I did not want to wait until I was 60 years old and had the approval of the communist party to pursue a doctoral degree.

I came to America because I wanted a better life for myself and for my children. I did not want to toil day and night under the watchful eye of the totalitarian government who decided how much our labor was worth and how much we were allowed to eat, where to travel, seek medical care, or live.

We knew there was a better place to live, a place called capitalism, a place called America, where they had freedom of speech and assembly. I knew there was a better life under capitalism where everybody had the opportunity to create wealth if they "served their fellow man" with needed products and services. I also knew that equal results were not guaranteed, only equal opportunity.

I did not want to live any longer under the failed socialist economy and the failed communist utopian ideology where wealth was stolen, property plundered, and the workers, "lovingly" called the proletariat, were enslaved with the false promise that the government will take care of them if they relinquished their most cherished possession – their freedom.

I wanted to own a home, no matter how small and I did not want it indebted to the government. I wanted proper medical care and medicine when needed for which I fully expected to pay. I did not feel entitled to anybody's wealth that I had nothing to do with creating.

I wanted freedom to exercise my faith if I so chose and be able to own or read a Bible. I wanted my children to learn historical truth, not revisionist communist indoctrination. I also did not want to yield to other religions imposed by the government whether be the worship of Gaia, atheism, environmentalism, or Islam.

I did not want free housing, free medical care, free child care, free cell phones, free education, and I certainly did not want to be indebted for generations to the federal government for my family's well-being. I did not want welfare and I expected to have as many children as I could afford to bring into this world, raise, support financially, and educate without the government's interference. I certainly did not expect political correctness to stifle my freedom of speech.

I came to America to escape having to march in May 1 (May Day) forced parades paying homage to the grand communist party. Yet now our President has proclaimed May Day "Loyalty Day," to "reaffirm our allegiance to the United States of America, our Constitution, and our founding values." Do we really need a loyalty day? Are we not loyal to our country already?

I must admit that I am a bit confused. Since the rest of the world celebrates May Day as a communist day, does this mean that we are joining in with the commies, or is it just an accidental and unfortunate coincidence that we celebrate loyalty to the United States, fly our flag, and pledge allegiance to our Republic on the same day?[43]

Listening to the Voice of America, the only radio of freedom news that we could covertly listen to under the oppressive communist regime, we held in high esteem the 100 Senators from the magical and free land of milk and honey, the United States. Unfortunately, living here as an American citizen, I must admit that I am shocked and puzzled by the bizarre behavior of some U.S. Senators and Representatives.

Take for instance Senator Dick Durbin (D-IL) who spoke on May Day in Chicago to a rally of "nearly two thousand trade unionists, open communists, socialists, anarchists and illegal aliens." He spoke of May Day as "Law Day." I must admit, I have never heard of such celebration, "Law Day."

Sen. Durbin, quoted by Rebel Pundit, said that, because he believes in free speech and the Constitution, he decided to come to "Law Day" rally attended by individuals who promoted the goals of communism. It is hard to believe - I fled communism 35 years ago and communism is following me to the United States, promoted by a U.S. Senator who also thinks that illegal immigration, breaking the laws of the country he swore to protect and defend, should be legalized because, he said, "My fellow immigrants, this is a once in a lifetime chance to get immigration reform." I wonder from what country did Senator Durbin immigrate illegally.[44]

We did "get" immigration reform in 1986 for 3 million illegal aliens and it did not work so well, we have gained since then 11 more million illegal immigrants. And they are still coming because the largesse of the American government towards invaders is world-renowned and their rights trump the rights of any American immediately upon arrival. All they have to do is "lawyer up." And financially, they are given a work permit immediately, a Social Security card, and the right to claim thousands of dollars in Earned

Income Tax Credit going three years retroactively, while American veterans die waiting in line to be seen at a Veterans hospital, or waiting to receive their promised and undelivered veteran benefits.

According to the Border Patrol, thousands of illegals have been apprehended since the administration and the Gang of Eight's announcement of amnesty has been made. CBS news reported that in McAllen, Texas, 900 illegals were caught over a three day period. In March, 7,500 illegals were arrested in the Rio Grande Valley of South Texas, more than triple from previous months.

Illegal immigration in the U.S. had slowed during our deep economic recession, particularly since Mexico's unemployment rate has held steady at 3.68 percent from 1994-2012. This prompted the American Border Control, the formerly U.S. Seaport Commission, a project of the U.S. Public Policy Council, to demand through its Executive Director, Jonathon Moseley, that U.S. citizens have the right to take jobs in Mexico. Moseley commented that "We are gullible suckers. The error of amnesty is the myth that Mexicans are in financial trouble."[45]

American Border Control is "demanding that any compromise include a right for unemployed U.S. citizens to find jobs in Mexico after losing their jobs in the United States as a result of Sen. Marco Rubio's policies." Executive Director Jonathon Moseley said that "Those who showed contempt for our country by violating our laws and crashing the gate should not be also stealing jobs from U.S. citizens."

Our President took an apology tour to Mexico to tout his immigration reform and shore up more Democrat voting support. He said, "It would provide a pathway to earned citizenship for the 11 million individuals who are already in this country illegally."

He apologized to Mexican college students for our sovereignty and thanked them for helping elect him President. Should Mexico not apologize to us for their lack of social responsibility to their citizens? Should Mexico not at least thank us for feeding, clothing, sheltering, educating, and treating medically for free millions of their citizens who sneak into our country illegally, becoming a burden to the U.S. taxpayers?

Balkanizing the United States by bringing in uneducated, often illiterate Mexicans and illegals from other countries that are hostile to our way of life and to our Christianity may not be such a good idea. Why not bring in educated immigrants and skilled workers who want to assimilate, learn English, who love America, and who want to make it better in the pursuit of the American dream? Why bring in uneducated Muslims from countries that despise our western culture and are Christophobic? Why not bring in legal immigrants that benefit and improve America, instead of turning it into a third world nation?

Perhaps instead of waiting 8 years to gain a green card and then my American citizenship, I should have crossed the southern border with Mexico illegally. It would have been quicker, I would have received immediate financial help to support myself instead of working, I would not have needed to learn English or assimilate, the government would have translated everything for me, given me free medical care, free education, easy citizenship, no waiting in line, earned income credit for other people's innumerable babies, and no uncomfortable interrogations and interviews.

Isn't self-suicidal, tolerant America grand? What other country in the world rewards law-breakers with citizenship for anchor babies, voting rights, free education, free housing, free health care, welfare, and chain migration? La Raza should be so proud! Our own officials are subtly or overtly promoting Reconquista of southern California, New Mexico, Arizona, and Texas.

I came to this country to find freedom and I did find it for a while. But the bright lights of "the shiny city on the hill" are getting dimmer day by day, and the "shiny city" is getting more tarnished with every new regulation, law, executive order, executive action, and proclamation that benefit illegals and other foreign hostile groups, and hurt American citizens.

Socialist Work Ethic

One of the first things that pleasantly surprised me about Americans upon my arrival in 1978 was the strong American work ethic, "the belief in work as a moral good." The Webster's Dictionary claims that the word "work ethic" was first used in 1951. I was contrasting it with the socialist workers' paradise work ethic I saw in my twenty years of life under the communist party regime – "we pretend to work and they pretend to pay us."

Daddy used to tell us stories about his young team of misfit apprentices who hid as soon as they arrived at work to continue their morning sleep. Dad had to look for them in new nooks and hideouts every day. It was a challenge and an irritation to get people to work because they could never be fired, no matter how bad they were. The communist party dictated that, in order to keep the masses quiet, everybody had to have a job and a meager salary. In their pursuit of a better hiding place, some hapless greenhorns crawled into dangerous areas with toxic fumes and liquids. Dad worked in a large refinery that had supplied oil to the German Army during World War II under another misguided regime.

The employment card each worker carried only showed a stamp with the place and time of employment – no room for work performance evaluation or any such capitalist "exploitation."

I was in awe at the long hours Americans worked, their dedication to the work place, productivity, personal responsibility for errors, much better remuneration based on merit, and pride in a job well done. I soon understood why – people could get fired for non-performance and inability to do the job in a timely manner. This is something that socialist countries like France, Italy, and Greece are not allowed to do by law.

Unfortunately, things have changed in the 37 years since I arrived in the United States. Half of the population subscribes to socialist welfare, work ethic long forgotten. Why try so hard to work when welfare, food stamps (EBT cards), disability, out of wedlock babies, and 99 weeks unemployment are so much more lucrative? Let the other 50 percent idiots go to work and earn distributive welfare income for the rest. Government taxation and income redistribution are very generous. All welfare recipients have to do is keep voting Democrat and the bonanza follows.

I am not sure if Americans arrived at this attitude because of our insane government largesse, with the help of the Democrats who promise more social justice, or because they have followed the lead of the European socialists. Surely they cannot believe that it is morally and socially just to steal from the labor of those who work and give it to those who prefer sloth. How can those on welfare have the gall to complain vociferously that the "rich do not pay their fair share," demanding "social justice" and "equality," when they receive unearned handouts from taxpayers, welfare they euphemistically and conveniently call "entitlements?"

The Greeks, for example, have exercised for years their political options based on self-interest. In codependent complicity with the political class, the welfare class changes their votes to the party that offers most goodies. If statistics are to be believed, 70 percent of the population receives some sort of benefit payment for partial or total handicap.

An old man lamented that "Greeks have forgotten how to work." Therefore a new mantra emerged, "Politicians pretend to govern and Greeks pretend to protest." Anarchy stoked from the far right and the far left gains more converts by using the mantra of pretend, nobody puts forth any real effort. Greeks seem to love anarchy because it is so financially profitable.

Tax cheats abound at the local and government levels. People don't like taxation and some successfully avoid paying taxes. The railroad borrows 700 million euros for daily operations and winds up with a 600 million deficit. The sink hole of the Greek economy is caused by collective duplicity, politicians, society, citizens without a work ethic, unions, business owners, and the European Union who turns a blind eye to all the corruption.

Greece is a good example of the deliberate demise of a country caused by the depreciating work ethic. Greece, once famous for its art, architecture, and military genius, is now infamous for its social, political, and economic bankruptcy. And they just voted a far left party into power that promised them that all austerity measures will be rejected.

The French work ethic was at the center of a spat between Titan International and the left-wing minister of industry, Arnaud Montebourg. Maurice Taylor, the CEO of Titan, sent a letter to Montebourg, which was made public in the Parisian press, in which he told him why Titan had no interest in buying a doomed Goodyear's Amiens Nord tire factory. "The French workforce gets paid high wages but works only three hours. They get one hour for breaks and lunch, talk for three and work for three."

Industry minister Montebourg replied that Taylor's comments were "extremist and insulting," particularly since French products are superior. "Mr. Taylor, saying he will pay a euro an hour to Chinese workers to give us crappy products, excuse my language, is unacceptable to our French farmers."

The chief of the French employers' union MEDEF, Laurence Parisot, injected his opinion in the debacle and said that Mr. Taylor's letter was "unacceptable." He admitted that there "were some irregularities in the French way of working, but generalizing it to the whole of France was 'shocking.'"

The Goodyear Tire and Rubber Co. of Amiens Nord faces closure because of disagreements between the union representing 1,250 workers and the management - employees must work more shifts or accept layoffs.[46]

The case of Fiat illustrates the work ethic of Italians, at least those in the southern part of Italy. After having "rescued" Chrysler, Sergio Marchionne of Fiat was hoping to convince workers to be more devoted to their jobs, to cut down on bad working habits such as calling in sick while working on another job in order to double their pay, or skip work with a fake doctor's excuse on the day a favorite soccer team plays a game.

Pormigliano d'Arco is the lowest performing plant of the Fiat Empire – it has operated at 32 percent capacity in 2008-2010. The 5,200 employees produce Alpha Romeos. Fiat did not close the plant because it would have destroyed almost 50 percent of the region's economy and the livelihood of 15,000 families in a very poor area with the highest unemployment in Italy, 20 percent less productivity, and prominent organized crime. "As Fiat goes, so goes Italy," and Italians like their "humane working life."

Nello Niglio, a factory worker, was quoted in the New York Times, criticizing Mr. Marchionne's requirements for longer work hours and less absenteeism. "He wants to impose American-style standards. But too much work is going to kill our workers."[47]

The socialist workers of Italy, Greece, or France are not giving up their life-long secured employment perks in order to adopt an American work ethic of responsibility, accountability, and decency. God forbid, they may die from overwork. Instead, Americans are adopting by the millions the socialist work ethic.

"A 57-year old well-educated alcoholic receives Social Security, free rent, free utilities, and free healthcare. He refuses to work. As soon as his check comes in, he goes straight to the liquor store."

"A share-cropper from Georgia, retired from Ford, still works at 77 and has a tremendous work ethic. His son, a strong, healthy young man of 44 only takes odd jobs for cash in the underground economy. He does not want an official paycheck because he has amassed a $75,000 college loan debt which he has no intention of paying back."

Men with welfare-mom girlfriends are well financed – they wear expensive clothes and drive nice cars. The "bread winner" in the family is often the young woman who keeps getting pregnant and having babies by different men who disappear into society, leaving the taxpayer-supported welfare system to care for their offspring. "This is the Democrat-voting constituency whose entitlement spending the current administration refuses to cut."

But then we should not call them entitlements, they are welfare, taxpayer-funded handouts. Social Security and Veterans benefits are entitlements because they were "earned and paid for by the recipients" or their immediate families.

I have worked 12-hour days my entire adult life and still do. I have not gotten sick from hard work, on the contrary, there was a sense of pride and accomplishment for a job well done, and I felt good to be able to pay my bills and take care of my family.

My friend, David S., a scientist with a Ph.D. and a businessman, has worked since he was six years old, delivering papers on a five-mile long route, crossing the busy Lincoln Highway two times. He also worked at the corner gas station during high school. The quintessential entrepreneur, David started his own lab at age 55 and made it a resounding success through hard work. He still labors 80 hours a week, including some bookkeeping, and has not been sick a day in 45 years. His European friends tell him that he could not start such a business in Europe because of regulations, bureaucracy, and the European mindset. Europeans do not want to work more than eight hours per day, no weekend work, prefer five-week vacations, national holidays off, a thirteenth salary, and other deserved and undeserved perks. Many European Union countries have switched to a 30-hour workweek.

American work ethic based on values of hard work and diligence has enhanced the moral character of millions. Americans with a strong work ethic are reliable, entrepreneurial, take initiative, and always pursue new skills and ventures. Traditionally, Americans with a good work ethic have been selected for better positions of responsibility and promoted more often.

In the last decades, however, a degradation of the moral character has resulted in a diminished work ethic. Promotions not based on merit but on ethnic, racial, and gender quotas further exacerbate the problem. The entitlement mentality that is now promoted by the main stream media and the government is pervasive in the country; it has driven more nails into the work ethic coffin, promoting the European socialism mindset and a dubious work ethic, alien to our American values. Our anemic economic recovery is the result of this mentality and of constant government regulations that are strangling entrepreneurship, innovation, creativity, and progress.

Faith Rises from the Ashes of the Soviet Communism

On a warm sunny day, September 7, 2011, cousin Ana drove us to the village of Popesti where my father was buried 22 years ago. I waited for this moment with bated breath to say hello and good-bye to my dad and place a wreath on his tomb.

We drove on the newly asphalted road up the beautiful hills covered with grape vines, the black grapes ripening in the fall sun. I recognized the river where we used to bathe as children, impervious to the dangers of the swift waters. None of us knew how to swim.

When the road ended, we parked and walked through the cobbled streets to the small cemetery, peaceful in its simplicity. A light breeze was swaying the tall blades of overgrown grasses and weeds. The mixture of marble, cement, metal, and wooden crosses was a forest of forgotten sadness against the backdrop of a picturesque valley, surrounded by smoky hills.

My grandmother walked with me every fall to those hills for the autumn fair to exchange hand-made goods and food with neighboring villagers. It seemed like such a far-away place to walk for a small child, but the excitement of the festive atmosphere and rides was more than enough to put an extra skip in my pace.

I expected a beautiful marble cross with dad's picture on it, as is the custom. We certainly paid a fortune to his brother to do so. Instead, I found a rotted wooden cross, barely holding together, dad's name long washed and faded by 25 years of rain, snow, and sunshine. Nearby was dad's marble cross with my grandparents' names engraved on it; they had died long time ago and their crosses had long disappeared.

I wept in sadness and despair at the fate, even in death, of my beloved Dad. He had carried a heavy cross most of his life under the repressive communism he despised. Yet in death, a dark, rotted piece of wood marked his grave instead of the beautiful marble cross we bought.

Dad passed away at the age of 61, beaten once too many times by the communist regime goons and left untreated in a hospital for almost thirty days. It was a torturous death, denied proper care and food. His sister Marcella did the best she could to care and comfort him.

I lit two candles and placed the wreath in sobbing silence, punctuated by a few chirping birds. I asked my dad for forgiveness that I could not save his life. I promised that I would return to place another marble cross with his name engraved and his photograph, as is the orthodox custom.

The church I attended as a child was in bad need of repairs. The villagers had a sizeable fund to restore it to its original beauty but it was hard to find an architect and workers. The fall of communism allowed people to worship overtly. Thousands of new churches were built and old ones restored. In time, this 20th century relic will be restored once more to its glory.

As we were leaving, the church bells were pealing in the distance very slowly, a sign that someone had died. When the bells rang faster, it was to announce to worshippers that a holiday was coming.

Restored Orthodox Church in Ploiesti

My baptism church

The maternal grandparent's village church where I was baptized had already been completely restored. Communists allowed the existence of some churches because they needed a place for baptisms, marriages, and burials. There were no funeral homes at the time. People could marry in a civil ceremony performed by a communist clerk at the city hall instead of a church.

St. John's Cathedral

I was happy to see that St. John's Cathedral, the church I said my marriage vows in on a cold January long time ago, was being completely restored.

The parish church close to our former tenement home was hidden behind a huge 15-story mixed-used high rise building Ceausescu had built on purpose to hide its existence. The dictator had become increasingly vicious in the last years of his reign, 1985-1989, and the Romanian people had become more desperate for a change that would improve their impoverished lives and the lack of food and freedom.

To make room for his grandiose, monstrous "People's Palace," the communist dictator demolished anything in its path, including old churches, some dating back to the 1400s. It was sad that so many centuries of beautiful architecture and faith were destroyed in order to make room for his personal residence, a bizarre ode to communism and elitist opulence while the masses were forced to starve for the good of the country.

I was pleased to see in the few bookstores we found, brand-new Bibles for sale. Open markets sold flowers, wreaths, and candles of all shapes and sizes. There was no longer a ban on worshipping and churches were full on weekends.

Faith has risen from the ashes of evil communism and is thriving everywhere in Romania. But progressives, communists, and socialists are getting stronger again, mesmerizing a new generation of people who have no knowledge or memory of the atrocities committed by the communists of the past. This new generation is accepting and embracing willingly the agenda of totalitarian control dressed in the empty suit of "social justice," "environmental justice," and "equality."

Notes

1. Newman, Alex, "South Africa Enters 'Second Phase of Communist Revolution," *The New American*, June 30, 2014 (http://www.thenewamerican.com/world-news/africa/item/18594-south-africa-enters-second-phase-of-communist-revolution).
2. Kengor, Paul, *Communism: Its Ideology, Its History, and Its Legacy*, Victims of Communism Memorial Foundation, 2013.
3. Meyer, Alfred G., *What You Should Know about Communism*, p.23, Harvard University Press, 1953.
4. Op-ed, "Agentes antirumores contra el racismo," *e-Noticies*, October 31,2011 (http://mas-ediciones.e-noticies.es/barcelones/agentes-antirumores-contra-el-racismo-58588.html).
5. Booker, Cristopher, "Sinister Groupthink Powers the Modern World, *The Telegraph*, May 24, 2014 (http://www.telegraph.co.uk/earth/environment/10853279/Sinister-groupthink-powers-the-modern-world.html).
6. Meyer, Alfred G., *How We Can Fight Communism*, chapter VII, p. 42, Harvard University Press, 1953.

7. *Draft of the Program of the Communist Party's Twenty-Second Congress of U.S.S.R*, Crosscurrents Press, New York, October 1961.
8. Ibid, p. 124.
9. Ibid, p. 112.
10. Ibid, p. 113.
11. Ibid, p. 119.
12. Ibid, p. 124.
13. Ibid, p. 9.
14. Ibid, p. 11.
15. Toosi, Mitra, "A Century of Change: The U.S. Labor Force, 1950-2050, *Bureau of Labor Statistics*, May Labor Review, 2002. (http://www.bls.gov/opub/mlr/2002/05/art2full.pdf).
16. *Draft of the Program of the Communist Party's Twenty-Second Congress of U.S.S.R.*, Crosscurrents Press, New York, October 1961, p. 65.
17. Ibid, p. 82.
18. Ibid, p. 74.
19. Ibid, p. 15.
20. Ibid, p. 21.
21. Ibid, p. 22.
22. Ibid.
23. Ibid, p. 25.
24. Ibid, p. 26.
25. Ibid.
26. Ibid, p. 27.
27. Ibid.
28. Ibid, pp. 28-29.
29. Ibid, p. 39.
30. Ibid, p. 50.
31. Ibid, p. 51.
32. Ibid.

33. Ibid, p. 108.
34. Ibid, p. 109.
35. Ibid, p. 84.
36. Ibid, pp. 90-91.
37. Reason TV, "How TV's 'Dallas' Won the Cold War," published June 15, 2012. (http://www.youtube.com/watch?v=-HZ4FNIn0VA)
38. McGeehon, Dale, "Former Romanian Describes Ceausescu's Reign of Brutality," *Times News*, Hendersonville, N.C., December 22, 1989 (http://news.google.com/newspapers?nid=1665&dat=19891222&id=eEgaAAAAIBAJ&sjid=1iQEAAAAIBAJ&pg=4888,6167293).
39. Barbu Laurentiu, identitatea.it, posted on October 27, 2013 (http://www.identitatea.it/foametea-din-basarabia-1946-1947/).
40. Moraru, Alexandru, "Canibalismul provocat the sovietici in Basarabia,Historia.ro, (http://www.historia.ro/exclusiv_web/general/articol/canibalismul-provocat-sovietici-basarabia).
41. Sony Pictures Classics, "The Lives of Others trailer," Youtube.com video uploaded on January 9, 2007 (http://www.youtube.com/watch?v=n3_iLOp6IhM).
42. www.ileanajohnson.com.
43. Presidential Proclamation, "Loyalty Day, 2014," The White House, May 1, 2014 (http://www.whitehouse.gov/the-press-office/2014/05/01/presidential-proclamation-loyalty-day-2014).
44. Chasmar, Jessica, "Sen. Dick Durbin defends his decision to address May Day rally," *The Washington Times*, May 2, 2013 (http://www.washingtontimes.com/news/2013/may/2/sen-dick-durbin-defends-his-decision-address-may-d/).
45. Moseley, Jon, Esq., Director, American Border Control, Freedom Leadership Conference, *"Legalize Illegals? 'Right to Work' in Mexico Demanded for U.S. Citizens,"* July 17, 2013 (www.AmericanBorderControl.org).

46. Dutton, Nick, "Good Year CEO's letter about French work ethic sparks fury," CBS News, February 28, 2013 (http://wtvr.com/2013/02/28/good-year-ceos-letter-about-french-work-ethic-sparks-fury/).

47. Aldeman, Liz, "Fiat Pushes Work Ethic at Italian Plant," The New York Times, July 22, 2010 (http://www.nytimes.com/2010/07/23/business/global/23fiat.html?pagewanted=all&_r=0).

About the Author

A former Economics college teacher with thirty years teaching experience, the author grew up in communist Romania during the brutal regime of Nicolae Ceausescu. She has the unique perspective of a totalitarian regime and values freedom and the opportunity for success that natural born Americans take for granted. She warns of the daily loss of freedoms that are threatening our sovereignty as the United Nations is attempting to dismantle America piece by piece, turning it into its "global" fiefdom.

A weekly segment radio commentator for Butler on Business, Liberty Express Radio, Silvio Canto Jr. Blog Talk Radio, and senior columnist for Canada Free Press, Fairfax Free Citizen, and Freedom Outpost, the author uses her extensive knowledge to inform thousands of readers and listeners. Because she speaks several languages and has taught four during her college career, Dr. Johnson Paugh can read the news as they happen around the globe.

Her previous books, "Echoes of Communism," "Liberty on Life Support," and "U.N. Agenda 21: Environmental Piracy" are available at Amazon in paperback and Kindle.

"Echoes of Communism" is a compilation of childhood experiences, describing the daily life in a totalitarian state: religion, superstitions, poverty, confiscation of property, social engineering, education, and lack of freedom of speech. She describes the harsh reality of communist life, not the romanticized version taught in American public schools and promoted by the main stream media.

"Liberty on Life Support" presents essays on American exceptionalism, education, the U.S. economy, and immigration, reflecting the massive destructive changes that took place in our country in the past four years.

"U.N. Agenda 21: Environmental Piracy" explains the profound impact the United Nation's Agenda 21 has on every facet of human life as NGOs are forcing all governments to redeploy human and financial resources in order to integrate every society under the aegis of the reviled United Nations, which will then abolish private property rights in the name of protecting the globe from environmental disasters caused by man-made climate change.

The author can be reached through her website, ileanajohnson.com, her Facebook author page, and her blog, Romanian Conservative.

Other Books by Dr. Ileana Johnson Paugh

Echoes of Communism
Lessons from an American by Choice

Liberty on Life Support
Essays on American Exceptionalism, Immigration, Education, and Economy

U.N. Agenda 21: Environmental Piracy
An in-depth look at all the facets of the Green Agenda

22757154R00104

Made in the USA
San Bernardino, CA
19 July 2015